101 Science Activities

for Emerging Einsteins

Written by Tracey Ann Schofield

Illustrated by Alex Glikin

Teaching & Learning Company

1204 Buchanan St., P.O. Box 10
Carthage, IL 62321-0010

This book belongs to

_____

Dedication and Thanks

This book is dedicated to anyone who has ever asked "why?"
and stubbornly sought an answer.
And to anyone who has ever been asked "why?" and struggled to provide one.

Thank you to all of those who have gone before and to all of those who will follow after.
This book is offered both as an acknowledgement of your pioneering efforts
and as a stepping-stone along the endless road to enlightenment.

Thanks also to Robynne Eagan for helping me to develop the framework for this book;
to Denise Shannon for lending me the contents of her extensive home science library;
to my family for helping me to transform our kitchen into a science lab; to my Mom for
proofreading my original manuscript; and to Judy Mitchell and Jill Day
for taking an interest in—and a chance on—my 101 ideas!

Table of Contents

Dear Teacher or Parent,

In simple terms, science is the study of the way things work and the reasons why they work that way. As such, scientific study is second nature to children, who are infinitely curious about the world around them and who, from a very early age, question everything with youthful enthusiasm and an apparently insatiable appetite for knowledge and understanding. Fortunately for these persistently inquisitive little souls, scientific principles underpin everything we see and do in our daily lives. We simply fail to appreciate its omnipresence. I wrote *101 Science Activities for Emerging Einsteins* to bring children face to face with the science that is inherent in their everyday activities.

The format of this book is unique. Although it provides children with the opportunity to explore the main branches of scientific study—life sciences or biology, the study of animals, plants and other living organisms; chemistry, the study of substances (their composition, characteristics and interactions with one another); physics, the exploration of forces, motion, heat and light; Earth sciences such a geology (the study of rocks and the Earth) and meteorology (the study of weather), which examine the Earth's development and its state of constant change; and astronomy, the study of stars, planets and other galactic phenomena—it does so in the context of an everyday science adventure. From waking to dressing to eating to thinking to playing to sleeping, *101 Science Activities for Emerging Einsteins* takes children on an extraordinary scientific journey through an ordinary day.

Each of the 101 activities carves the scientific process into manageable slices. I Spy Science challenges children to question everyday occurrences; Science at Work provides them with straightforward but provocative experiments and the opportunity to observe, hypothesize and deduce; and Simple Science offers an easy-to-understand explanation of what happened and why. Additional experiments are suggested under Science Stuff. Sentimental Science and Suggestive Science link science to the English curriculum by examining the relationship between the language of science and the common vernacular and reinforces the principles of purpose and creative writing by encouraging children to pen their personal experiences. Finally, Science Stunners offers tantalizing tidbits of useful knowledge and fascinating facts.

The tried and tested experiments in this book can be performed at school or at home, in serial or random fashion, using simple materials that can be found around the house or purchased inexpensively at the grocery store or drugstore. Although young scientists can do much of the hands-on experimenting in this book without adult supervision, educators and parents should reinforce some fundamental principles and basic rules before turning students loose in the classroom or kitchen lab:
- Always get permission from an adult in charge before conducting an experiment.
- Be careful! Part of being a scientist is being responsible in your pursuit of knowledge. Make safety—yours and that of others—a top priority.
- Be sure to clean up after an experiment and dispose of materials properly.

- Read all of the instructions and check the "you will need" list before starting an experiment so that you know, up-front, what you need and what you have to do.
- Expect the unexpected. Don't be disappointed if the results of an experiment are not what you thought they would be. That's science. Repeat the experiment. If you are still disappointed, try to determine why things went wrong. Not everything you attempt will be a success, but finding out what doesn't work is just as important as finding out what does.
- Don't be afraid to make minor alterations and slight adjustments. Modify experiments—even create your own—but be sure to keep notes. The "trial and error" approach is at the heart of the scientific process and many of the world's great discoveries.
- Look at the world around you. Try to observe examples of the scientific principles that you have learned during your experimentation.
- Never stop asking why.

You don't have to be a scientist or even know much about science to have fun exploring the world around you and to find wonder in everyday things. All you need is the willingness to see and the desire to know. Writing *101 Science Activities for Emerging Einsteins* changed the way I look at, experience and make sense of my immediate environment. As a result, I am much less likely to take anything for granted and find myself involuntarily searching out the "whats" and "whys" in everything I do. I hope that this book helps you and your children to embrace the adventure and have as much fun *discovering the science* in your daily lives as did I.

Sincerely,

Tracey

Tracey Ann Schofield

Just Like Clockwork

I Spy Science

Have you ever woken up panicky, your heart pounding in your chest, your stomach clenching at the thought that you might have overslept and missed an important event—only to find that you are actually awake right on time or even earlier than you need to be?

Simple Science

Do you find that you wake up at just about the same time every day? Your clock radio might not be beeping or singing at you, but that doesn't mean your alarm system has failed you. We all have an internal clock that keeps us ticking, maintaining regular patterns of involuntary behavior—breathing, blinking, swallowing, sleeping, etc. The sleep/wake cycle is programmed according to one of these biological or body clocks.

Science at Work

Try this simple experiment to test your biological sleep/wake clock. Don't set the alarm before you go to bed and ask your family members to let you sleep until your body tells you that it's time to wake up. (You'll have to set a maximum sleep limit or try this while you're on holiday to make sure you're not late for school!) Repeat this several days in a row. Do you wake up at roughly the same time every day? Does your body reset its sleep/wake clock for the weekend?

Sentimental Science

• Describe your normal wake-up routine.

Science Stunner

• Scientists have found that in mice, the sleep/wake clock is genetically programmed. Because every living creature inherits its gene set from its parents, that means that the sleep/wake program is passed down from one generation of mice to the next.

Breathe in; Breathe Out

I Spy Science

Are you breathing right now? Of course you are. You breathe all the time as air passes in and out of your nose. Like your sleep/wake cycle, your breathing is also controlled by a biological clock. Unless something goes terribly wrong with your body or brain, respiration (breathing) occurs regularly and continuously 24/7.

Science at Work

To simulate the inhale/exhale action of your lungs during breathing, you will need a plastic bottle, a drinking straw, modeling clay, two rubber bands, two balloons, scissors and tape.

Ask an adult to cut the bottom off the plastic bottle. Snip the narrow neck off one balloon. Stretch the balloon over the bottom of the bottle, secure with a rubber band and tape in place. Put the end of the straw into the second balloon and hold it in place with the other rubber band. Again, use tape to hold the straw in place. Wrap some clay around the middle of the straw. Push the clay into the opening of the bottle so that the balloon hangs down inside. (Make sure the clay fits snugly in the opening so that air cannot pass in or out.) Holding the neck of the bottle, pull down on the bottom balloon and then release. What happens to the balloon inside the bottle?

Simple Science

Pulling on the bottom balloon causes the balloon inside the bottle to inflate. The inner balloon deflates when you release the bottom balloon. It is changes in volume (an increase, then a decrease) and pressure (a decrease, then an increase) that cause the air to move in and out of the inner balloon. Your lungs work in a similar fashion.

At rest, your two lungs hold about one-half gallon (2.5 liters) of air (they can hold more than one gallon [5 liters] when the body is very active). To collect oxygen for the body, your diaphragm

(a muscular partition that separates the chest from the abdomen) contracts, becoming shorter and flatter, and your lungs expand, stretching downwards. Your intercostals (the short muscles between each pair of ribs) contract, pulling up your ribs and stretching the lungs forward. All of this increases the volume of your chest cavity and decreases the pressure inside it. Because the air pressure outside of your body is greater than the pressure inside your chest cavity, air rushes in through your nose. When your diaphragm and intercostal muscles relax–pushing up and in–your spongy lungs scrunch together, decreasing the volume of your chest cavity and increasing the pressure inside it. This forces the old, stale air (which has been collected by the blood) out of your lungs and back out through your nose.

Science Stunner

- When you breathe you inhale (along with traces of other gases): nitrogen (78%), oxygen (21%) and carbon dioxide (0.04%) and exhale: nitrogen (79%), oxygen (16%) and carbon dioxide (4%).

Hold That Breath!

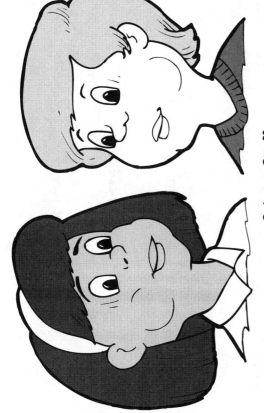

I Spy Science

There's a bad smell in your bedroom. Can you put your breathing on hold until it's gone?

Science at Work

Try holding your breath. How many seconds tick by before your body forces you to inhale? Is there any way you can increase the amount of time you can hold your breath?

Simple Science

Although you can prevent yourself from breathing for short periods of time—you do it all the time when you swim underwater—your breathing clock cannot be stopped. The human body has no way of storing oxygen, so it needs a constant, fresh supply to stay healthy. Two sensors situated near the large blood vessels that supply blood to your neck check the amount of oxygen in the blood that is going to your brain. If the oxygen level in your blood drops below a certain critical point and your brain is not getting the oxygen it needs—like when you are holding your breath—the sensors send out a distress signal. Your brain receives the alarm and forces you to breathe (or speed up your breathing if, for example, you are exercising strenuously). Although you can't stop the clock altogether, it is possible to increase your breath-holding capacity slightly. If you breathe in and out several times before you hold your breath, you put extra oxygen into your blood. Your cells can hang on a little longer with that additional extra oxygen, so you don't have to breathe as soon as you otherwise would.

Science Stuff

When you pull air in through your nose (which also has the job of warming and moistening the air and filtering out bits of dust with hairs and mucus), it goes down your throat and into your windpipe. The windpipe branches into two air tubes, the bronchi, which lead to the left and right lungs. In the lung, each bronchus divides into lots of smaller tubes, called bronchioles. Each bronchiole ends in 250 million microscopic bubbles, called alveoli. The alveoli are surrounded by superhighways of microscopic blood vessels called capillaries. Oxygen passes from the alveoli into the blood in the capillaries and is pumped around your body by the heart muscle.

Science Stunners

• Most people breathe 14–16 times each minute.
• Your brain is hungry for oxygen. It takes just under 3 cubic inches (46 cubic cm) of oxygen from the 166 pints (750 ml) of blood that flow through it each minute. That accounts for roughly 20 percent of the body's total at-rest oxygen consumption. Without oxygen, cells begin to die within minutes.

Alive and Breathing

I Spy Science

You know that you breathe—and so does your dog or cat or hamster. But what about your houseplants?

Science at Work

To prove that plants respire, you will need: a small, leafy plant and petroleum jelly.

Find a small leafy plant. (If you are using a plant that belongs to somebody else, make sure that you get permission from the plant's owner before you begin your experiment.) Choose four or five healthy looking leaves and coat their topsides with a thick layer of petroleum jelly. Spread petroleum jelly on the undersides of four or five other healthy leaves. Observe the plant for a week. What happens to the leaves? Why?

Simple Science

Plants "breathe" too. Not in the same way we do—they have leaves instead of lungs, for one thing—but like us their survival also depends on the regular exchange of air. Plants have special openings on the undersides of their leaves. The plant "breathes" as air passes in and out of these openings.

Science Stunner

- All living things respire. A fish breathes through gills, the red, blood-rich feathery things you can see under the slits on either side of its head. Like human lungs, gills take in oxygen. But while our lungs get oxygen from the air in a gaseous form, gills absorb oxygen that is dissolved in water. Bugs don't have lungs, either. But they still breathe in and out—through tiny holes in the sides of their bodies called spiracles.

Nothing but Blue Sky

I Spy Science

If you're lucky, today will be a bright, beautiful day with nothing but blue sky as far as the eye can see. Hey! Why is the sky blue, anyway?

Simple Science

Clear light is made up of all the colors in the rainbow—red, orange, yellow, green, blue, indigo and violet. These colors travel in waves. When the waves of color hit things, some of the colors are absorbed and others are reflected. The waves that are reflected and bounce back to your eyes are the colors that you see. Far above your head on sunny days, waves of light hit the air. The air is made up of tiny gas molecules. The blue light waves bounce off these molecules and scatter across the sky. So, when you look up, it's nothing but blue sky.

Sentimental Science

- Describe your favorite blue thing. Why do you think your favorite blue thing is, well, blue?

Suggestive Science

- Why do we say that people are blue when they are feeling sad?
- How does the color blue make you feel?

Get a Move On

I Spy Science

You're awake! The good news is that you're breathing. The bad news is that you have to get out of bed. Groan. It is a scientific rule (called inertia): unless something forces it to move, an object at rest tends to stay at rest. And you are definitely at rest.

Science at Work

To witness inertia, "inaction," you will need a strip of paper, a ruler, a handful of pennies and a counter or tabletop.

Place one end of the paper on a table or counter and place a stack of pennies on it. Hold the loose end of the paper in one hand and quickly hit the paper with a ruler somewhere between your fingers and the table or counter edge. What happens to the pennies? Make the stack bigger. Make it smaller. Make a number of penny stacks. Do any of these changes alter the outcome of the experiment?

Simple Science

Inertia is the property of all things that makes them resist any change in their motion or to stay at rest until some outside force makes them move. When an object (your body) is standing (or lying) still, it takes force to get it moving. Once it is moving, however, it takes force to stop it. The heavier the object (and the greater its speed), the more force–or time–it takes to change its momentum.

At the beginning of the experiment, both the piece of paper and the pennies were at rest (actually, so was your hand and the ruler!). The ruler provided enough force to change the momentum of the light piece of paper and make it move, but not enough force to change the momentum of the pile of pennies. They stayed in place.

Sentimental Science

- How much force does it take to get you out of bed in the morning, to get you to take out the garbage, to get you to start your homework or stop watching TV?
- We often talk about "building up momentum." If you built up enough social momentum to do more than you already do in an average day, what good deeds or public service works would you do on behalf of your fellow human beings?

Science Stunner

- Of course, it takes some serious brain/body teamwork to overcome your morning inertia and get you up and moving. At the brain's command, your (640) muscles, (206) bones and joints all work together to make the body move.

Activity 7

Rise and Shine!

I Spy Science

The sun always rises in the east and sets in the west, but it seems to come up and go down at different places throughout the year. Why is that?

Science at Work

To find out, you will need two open areas, one facing east, the other west, a sketch pad and pencil.

To see how the sun apparently alters its rising and setting points, you will have to make some early morning and late evening observations at least four times over the course of a year. To get started, find an open area where you can make your observations. (You must stand in this same exactly spot each time you check the sun's position.) Make two sketches, one of the eastern horizon and one of the western horizon. Make sure to draw and label familiar and recognizable landmarks in your sketches. Make three copies of each sketch. Track the movement of the sun by recording its rising and setting positions on or close to (you might have to wait for a weekend) January 1, April 1, July 1 and October 1. In the morning, use one of your eastern sketches to mark the spot where the sun first pokes its shining face over the horizon. In the evening, use one of your western sketches to mark the spot where the sun finally dips below the skyline. Compare your four sketches.

NOTE: DO NOT LOOK DIRECTLY AT THE SUN. DOING SO–EVEN FOR JUST A FEW SECONDS–CAN DAMAGE YOUR EYES. TO MAKE YOUR OBSERVATIONS, GLANCE QUICKLY TOWARDS THE HORIZON WHEN THE TIP OF THE SUN IS JUST VISIBLE.

Simple Science

Although it looks like the sun has moved, it's really the Earth! Our planet is tilted toward the sun on its axis. As the Earth moves around (orbits) the sun over the course of one full year, the degree of that tilt changes. As a result, the sun rises and sets at different points along the horizon.

Science Stunners

- The surface temperature of the sun, is 10,832°F (6000°C)–60 times the boiling point of water–and it's even hotter at the center: an incredible 59 million°F (15 million°C).
- The sun is almost 869,565 miles (1.4 million km) across. It is so big that it pulls every object within about 3727 million miles (6000 million km) into orbit around it. The sun is so big that more than one million planets the size of the Earth would fit into it.

Me and My Shadow

I Spy Science

Have you ever noticed that dark, featureless guy or girl that kind of runs ahead of you or follows you around on bright, sunny days? Of course you have. That's your shadow. But why does he come and go, and how come she gets bigger and smaller?

Science at Work

To learn about your shadows, you will need a tape measure, a journal, a pencil and a friend.

To study the effect of the sun's position on your shadow, keep a shadow journal on a bright, sunny day. You will have to start first thing in the morning and record your observations until the sun goes down. Every hour on the hour, ask a friend to measure the length and width of your shadow. Mark the position of your shadow in your journal with each dimensional entry. What happens to your shadow over the course of the day? Why? When is it the biggest? When is it the smallest?

Simple Science

A shadow is something that is where light isn't. Light can do lots of things, but it can't travel through solid objects. On a bright, sunny day, light streams all around you and touches the ground. But when your body gets in the way of the light, it can't pass through. The dark spot that forms on the ground –your shadow–is the place where the light just can't reach.

Although your shadow follows–or leads–you everywhere, it isn't always the same size and shape. That's because the Earth is moving, and the position of the sun changes through-

out the day. When the sun is behind your back, your shadow appears in one place and when the sun is in your face, it appears somewhere else. Your shadow lengthens as your body gets further and further away from the sun. And what about when the sun is directly overhead?

Science Stuff

- Ask a friend to trace the outline of your shadow in chalk on the pavement or with a marker on a large piece of paper. Add your features to your shadow portrait.
- Make some shadow puppets by cutting shapes out of black construction paper and taping them to craft sticks. Put on a shadow puppet play in a lighted room or in a dark room in front of a flashlight beam. How many different shadow characters can you create using just your hands?

Activity 9

It's Raining; It's Pouring

I Spy Science

Uh, oh. What happened to that beautiful, sunny day the weatherperson (meteorologist) was calling for? It's raining; it's pouring—again.

Science at Work

To make it rain in your kitchen, you will need a large spoon, a kettle of boiling water and an adult's assistance.

Put the spoon in the freezer and leave it for half an hour. Just before you remove the spoon, ask an adult to put some water in a kettle and heat it. When the water is boiling, have the adult hold the freezing cold spoon in the water vapor. What happens?

Simple Science

As the liquid water in the kettle heats, it is converted to steam. When the steam leaves the kettle and comes into contact with the outside air, it cools and condenses, forming water vapor—the white stuff that comes out of the spout of your kettle. (Surprise! That white stuff is not steam. Steam is invisible. If you look carefully between the spout of the kettle and the misty water vapor, you will see a thin, clear space. That's steam.) When the water vapor hits your cold spoon, it cools and condenses into water—which produces a little rainstorm right in your kitchen.

In nature, rain occurs in much the same way. The heat from the sun warms the water in our laundry hanging on the line, in our puddles and in our rivers, lakes and oceans. The heat is not intense enough to boil the water (thank goodness!), but it is sufficient to allow tiny water molecules to evaporate (change from a liquid to a gas) and rise up into the sky. As the warm, water-filled air rises, it cools, and a cloud of water vapor forms. Because cold air can't hold as much water as warm air, some of the water condenses and falls back to Earth as rain or snow.

Sentimental Science

- Write about a time when rain spoiled your plans or when you got caught–and soaked–in an unexpected shower.

Science Stunner

- The cycling of the Earth's water has been going on since our planet was first formed. No new water is ever created: it is just continually cycled through nature. Believe it or not, you are drinking the same water that the dinosaurs did millions of years ago! Water is a precious natural resource, and that is why is it so important to take care of our lakes, rivers and oceans and keep them free of pollutants.

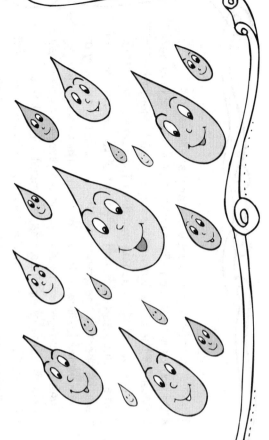

Activity 10

Water: Easy Come, Easy Go

I Spy Science

Look at all that rain collecting in puddles on the road. Where does it go after the storm?

Simple Science

Those puddles are part of the water cycle. Once the storm has passed and the sun comes out, the water in the puddles will heat up and evaporate into the air as water vapor. Up in the clouds, the tiny water droplets will start to join together. When the droplets become too heavy, they will fall to the Earth once again as rain, creating fresh puddles in the road.

Science at Work

You can observe and track the movement of water through the water cycle by making your own rain–or precipitation/evaporation–gauge. You will need a clear plastic jar or container with straight sides and a flat bottom, a ruler, clear tape, a journal, a pencil and an outdoor space that is open to the rain and sun.

To make your precipitation/evaporation gauge, tape the ruler to the container so that the bottom of the ruler sits on the ground and the numbers rise vertically up the jar. Place your gauge in a suitable outdoor space. (Make sure the jar is secured and will not tip over in the wind.) Record the water level in the jar every couple of days over the course of a season. What happens to the water level when it rains? What happens to the water level during a dry spell?

Science Stunners

- Do you know why it smells so fresh outside after it rains? Because the air is wet and clean, just like laundry when it comes out of the washing machine! The rain washes little bits of dust and soot and pollen out of the air and sort of sticks them to the ground so they don't get in the way of your nose smelling other, nicer things. The wet air carries fresh smells–like earth and grass and trees–to your nose better than dry air does, and the moist air makes the inside of your nose wetter so that it can trap those fresh smells more easily.

- There are as many as 15 million droplets of water vapor in one raindrop.

- Scientists estimate that 40 million gallons of water fall on the Earth every second of every day–in the form of rain, snow or freezing rain.

- One square mile of rain one inch (2.5 cm) thick weighs 72,000 tons.

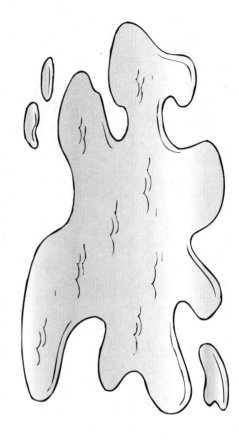

Activity 11

Killer Rain

I Spy Science

The meteorologist warned you about the rain, so you know to take an umbrella with you for protection on your way to school. But it will take more than an umbrella to protect you from the effects of acid rain.

Science at Work

To see how plants are affected by acidic rain (rain that has a lower-than-usual pH), you will need 3 potted plants (same variety and size), 3 spray bottles, water and vinegar.

Put your plants side by side in a nice sunny spot. Label the plant pots and the spray bottles as follows: *Rain, Acidic Rain, Extremely Acidic Rain.* Use straight tap water to fill the first bottle. Fill the second bottle 1/3 full of vinegar, and top it up with tap water. Fill the third bottle 2/3 full of vinegar and top it up with tap water. Record your baseline observations about the three plants: how tall are they, how do they appear? Spritz each plant every day over the next month with water from the corresponding spray bottle. Record your observations weekly. How does the "rain" affect each plant?

Simple Science

Because carbon dioxide in the air dissolves in rain to form carbonic acid, rainwater has always been slightly acidic. As more of the world has become industrialized, however, our rain has become more acidic. This is because fossil fuels, such as coal, release sulfur dioxide and nitrogen oxide when they are burned. These poisonous gases dissolve in the water droplets

in clouds and form sulfuric and nitric acid. Incorporated into the water cycle they return to Earth as acid rain or snow, damaging plant and wildlife in every ecosystem into which they fall.

Science Stunners

- Most of the sulfur dioxide in the air comes from power station emissions, while most of the nitrogen oxide in the air can be attributed to power stations and road traffic. (Commerce, homes, industry and refineries are other, lesser, culprits.)

- It is not only plants and animals that are harmed by acid rain. Stone, especially limestone (or calcium carbonate, which is broken down into carbon dioxide gas by acids), is also adversely affected. Acid rain can crumble statues and entire buildings.

- Because the wind can carry gases long distances, pollution produced in one country can fall as acid rain in another.

The Acid Test

I Spy Science

Is there acid in the rain that falls on your home and school and skin and dog?

Science at Work

To see if your local rain is acidic, you will need red cabbage, boiling water, strainer, container, white construction paper, lemon juice, tap water and rainwater.

Cut the cabbage in half and boil one half for three hours. Strain the cabbage water into a container. Once the water has cooled, use it to soak three 6" x 1" (15 x 2.5 cm) strips of construction paper. Lay the strips flat to dry. Dip one dry strip in lemon juice, one in tap water and one in rainwater.

Simple Science

The strips are acid testers. The pinker the strip after dipping, the more acidic the liquid in which it was dipped. Remember, lemon juice contains a weak acid–citric acid. If your rainwater strip is darker than lemon juice strip, should you be alarmed?

Suggestive Science

• In Latin, the word acid means "sour." Some people are described as having an acidic personality. What do you think this means?

Science Stunners

• Stinging ants produce methanoic (or formic) acid. At one time, people made formic acid–which is used to preserve crops stored for animal feed and to make paper and textiles–by boiling ants in a large pot.

• Your stomach contains hydrochloric acid, which kills germs in your food and helps break down proteins. Your stomach lining protects you from the ill effects of this strong acid.

• Acids are dangerous to living things, and because of this some can be used as preservatives to kill bacteria and keep food from going bad. Vinegar, used in pickling preserves such as cucumbers, is ethanoic or acetic acid.

• It is acid, present in small amounts, that turns white paper yellow–or even brown–over time.

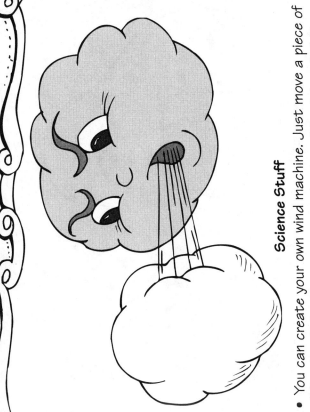

Windward Ho!

I Spy Science

There's more than rain happening today. What is making the branches of the trees sway like that, and why does your hair keep whipping into your face when you brush it back?

Simple Science

The force that you see and feel is called wind. But what causes wind? As the sun warms the surface of the Earth, the air just above the surface heats up. This warm air expands, becomes lighter and rises. As the warm, light air moves up and out, it creates an area of low pressure. Colder, heavier air sweeps in to take its place. This colder air then warms and rises and the cycle continues. At night, the air cools and becomes heavy. Because cooler air is heavier than warmer air, it falls, creating another area of low pressure that must be filled. It is this circular movement of air current that we call wind. The greater the difference between areas of high and low pressure the stronger the wind will be.

Science at Work

You can create a wind current in your own bedroom. You will need a lamp (with the shade removed) and talcum (baby) powder. Turn on the lamp. In a few minutes (when the bulb gets hot), sprinkle a pinch of talcum powder just above it. What happens? Just like wind in nature, the heat from the light bulb created a current of rising warm air. The talcum powder was carried upward on this artificial "wind."

Science Stuff

- You can create your own wind machine. Just move a piece of cardboard or folded newspaper back and forth in a fan-like motion near your face. Do you feel a breeze? That is wind! As the fan pushes the air in front of you out of its way–creating an area of low pressure–air from the surrounding area of higher pressure rushes in to take its place.

Science Stunner

- Winds that always happen at the same time or in the same place are given special names. Here are a few: Bhoots and Elephantas (India), Brickfielders (Australia), Chinooks (United States and Canada), Fohns (Europe), Doldrums (near the equator), Haboobs and Simooms (Africa), Kwats (China), Mistrals (Spain and France), Williwaws (Alaska), Xlokks (Malta), Zondas (Argentina).

Sentimental Science

- If you could name the wind that blows in your community, what would you call it?
- Write the first paragraph of a story about a very blustery day.

Hear Me Out

I Spy Science

Okay. You're awake. You're breathing. You've scoped the weather. Now you . . . Hey! Is that someone calling your name from the kitchen? How does that voice travel from one part of your home to another? How can you hear it?

Science at Work

To demonstrate how your ears work, you will need a piece of plastic wrap, a metal bowl, a rubber band, some cereal flakes, a cookie sheet and a wooden spoon.

Stretch the plastic wrap tightly over the top of the bowl. Use the rubber band to keep the plastic wrap in place. Sprinkle about 10 cereal flakes on top of the plastic wrap. Stand close to the bowl and bang the cookie sheet with the wooden spoon. What happens to the flakes of cereal?

Simple Science

When you hit the cookie sheet, the air molecules next to it were pushed out of the way. These molecules pushed against other air molecules, which pushed against other air molecules, creating a chain reaction of movement that travelled all the way to the bowl. This movement of air molecules created invisible sound waves, or vibrations, that moved through the air. When the vibrations hit the plastic wrap, they caused it to vibrate, too, and that made the cereal move. When you struck the cookie sheet, the sound waves travelled to your ears and made your eardrums vibrate.

Science Stuff

- Make a tape recording of your voice. Now play it back. Does it sound different than you would expect? Why? We are used to hearing our voice through the bones of our head—before it has a chance to go anywhere else. But when we hear our recorded voice, we're hearing it after the sound waves have already travelled through the air. Your tape-recorded voice is actually closer to the real you, at least the you that other people are used to hearing.

Science Stunners

- Sound travels at about 740 miles per hour (330 meters per second). That's almost as fast as a fighter jet!
- The tiniest bones in your body are in your inner ear. Commonly named after their shapes, the bones in your ear—the hammer (malleus—23 mg), the anvil (incus—25 mg) and the stirrup (stapes—2-4 mg)—transmit sound from the eardrum to the inner ear. (For reference: one milligram is equal to 35 millionths of an ounce!)

TLC10301 Copyright © Teaching & Learning Company, Carthage, IL 62321-0010

Activity 15

Speak to Me

I Spy Science

We know how we hear, but how do we speak? How did the person in the kitchen make the sounds that travelled to your bedroom and into your ears?

Science at Work

Make an "ahhh" sound in your throat. While you are making the sound, gently touch your fingers to your throat. Do you feel anything? Look in a mirror. While making your "ahhh" sound, move your lips, tongue, mouth and cheeks to make different sounds (o, e, l, y, m, etc.).

Simple Science

To make a sound, you push air from your lungs up and out of your mouth. On the way to your mouth, the air must pass between the vocal cords in your voice box (larynx). These cords are like the strings of a guitar or a rubber band stretched between your fingers: they stretch and move, and the tighter they stretch, the higher the sound produced. To vocalize (make a sound), the laryngeal muscles in your neck pull your vocal cords together so there is hardly any gap between them. When air flows past the vocal cords, it makes them vibrate and this vibration gives an extra push to the air molecules in your mouth. When the vibrating air molecules leave your mouth, they pass their vibrations along to all the air molecules in the room. When the vibrating air in the room reaches other people, it jiggles their eardrums and they can hear you. The vibrations from the vocal cords themselves are quiet and indistinct. We use our mouth, lips, teeth, tongue and cheeks to make the sounds and words that we speak out loud for others to hear and understand.

Science Stunner

• During normal breathing, the vocal cords, two flaps at the side of the larynx (which is at the top of the windpipe), gap open to form the glottis.

Hair Today, Gone Tomorrow

I Spy Science

Before you head to the kitchen for breakfast, you'd better take a quick look in the mirror. How's your "do"—your hairdo that is?

Science at Work

Sure, it's fun to style and great to look at, but there's more to your hair than you might think. To find out what your hair does for you (aside from minimizing the risk of sunburn!), you will need two glasses, hot tap water, a small towel, three rubber bands, two bowls of ice water and a clock or watch.

Fill both glasses with hot tap water. Wrap the towel tightly around one of the glasses, and hold it in place with the rubber bands. Set each glass in a bowl of ice water. Wait about 10 minutes; then dip the fingers of your left hand in one glass and the fingers of your right hand in the other. Is there a difference in water temperature between the two glasses?

Simple Science

Mammals (including humans) are warm-blooded, which means that the temperature inside their bodies stays the same all the time. And mammals (including humans) have hair or fur on their bodies to keep them warm in cold weather. The human body is designed to maintain a constant internal temperature of 98.6°F (37°C)—and that is the temperature at which you think and work your best. There are a number of body systems and special features that work together to keep your internal temperature steady, and your hair is one of them.

The water in the glass with the towel wrapped around it was warmer than the water in the glass that was not insulated against the cold. That's because the towel helped to keep the water in the glass warm. The towel, like your hair, helped to keep the heat in and the cold out. Your hair is an important insulator and plays a significant role in temperature regulation. And that's important when you find yourself out in the cold, since as much as 90% of your body heat escapes through your head!

More Simple Science

Have you ever wanted to be a detective? All you need is a magnifying glass (or microscope) and one generously donated piece of hair from each member of your household. On a white sheet of paper, tape and label each hair sample. Then scour the house for stray hairs. (If the carpet doesn't yield anything, try a hairbrush.) Using the magnifying glass, examine your labelled samples and compare them to the new specimen. Can you identify the owner of the missing hair?

Science Stunners

- Your hair tells a lot about you. Using a microscope, scientists can examine a hair to determine your age, sex and race.
- You have about five million hairs growing on your body. Of those, brunettes have about 155,000 scalp hairs; blondes have about 140,000; and redheads about 85,000.
- Some hairs are very visible, others are so small you would need a magnifying glass to see them! Only the soles of your feet and the palms of your hands are hairless.
- Each of your hairs grows from its own follicle (a deep pit in your skin). The follicle produces cells. As new cells grow, they push the older cells upward. That's what makes the hair grow.

Super Supple

I Spy Science

Other than moisturizing lotion, what keeps your skin soft?

Science at Work

To solve the soft skin mystery, you will need petroleum jelly, a paper towel and water.

Rub a thick layer of petroleum jelly into a small section of your paper towel. How does the treated paper towel feel compared to the untreated towel? Place a drip of water on the treated paper towel. Observe what happens. Place a drip of water on an untreated part of the towel. What happens?

Simple Science

Your skin secretes a mix of oils and waxes. This sebum comes from tiny sebaceous glands just under the skin's surface. Sebum can cause pimples, but you wouldn't want to live without it. Like the petroleum jelly, sebum makes your skin soft and water-resistant. If you didn't have it, your skin would crack like an old leather shoe—and soak up water in the bath like the untreated piece of paper towel.

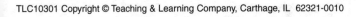

Activity 16 continued

- It is the cells in the follicle, not the hair, that are alive. Hair is made up of dead cells that are filled with keratin (a protein) and melanin (a brown pigment). The more melanin your hair contains, the darker your hair will be.

- After up to six years of growing a hair, follicles take a three-month rest. During the rest phase, the hair falls out of the follicle (you lose up to 125 hairs from your scalp every day). When the cells in the follicle become active again, a new hair starts to grow.

- Right now, 85% of your head of hair is growing, 15% is resting.

- Hair follicles on different parts of your body are programmed with different growth phases. Maximum hair length is determined by the length of the follicle's growth phase. Scalp hair can grow from two to six years. Eyelash hairs grow more slowly than scalp hairs, and they grow for only about four months before new hairs replace them.

- Most scalp hairs grow about 0.08 inches (2 mm) per week or 4.16 inches (10.4 cm) a year. The longest hair you could expect to grow would be about 25 inches (62.5 cm): (6 years x 4.16 inches/10.4 cm/yr = 25 inches/62.5 cm).

- Your hair will turn gray when you get older because the cells at the root of the hair, which produce pigment, gradually die off as you age.

- Balding occurs when your hair follicles start shrinking (due to hormonal changes) and cannot produce new hairs. Both men and women lose hair density as they grow older, but far more men than women go completely bald. "Male pattern baldness," is typical and is caused by the male hormone, testosterone.

Sentimental Science

- Describe your worst haircut or your best bad hair day!

Put on a Healthy Face

I Spy Science

How about that sleepy face? You might want to give it a little morning scrub to freshen up and get rid of a nighttime worth of oil, dead skin and bacteria.

Science at Work

What would happen to your body if you had no skin? Try this experiment to get an idea. You will need an apple and an apple peeler or knife.

Ask an adult to peel your apple. Leave the apple on the counter for as long as you can stand it. What happens to the apple?

Simple Science

If you did not have that 1/10 of an inch (.25 cm) of skin covering your body, your fatty and fleshy underlayers would be exposed to the elements. Much like the apple, your body fluids and salts would leak away or evaporate and dust and dirt would stick to you. Germs and bacteria—even mold—could gain easy entry to your body. You might become scaly on the outside, like a reptile! And you would have little or no protection against bumps, cuts and bruises, not to mention environmental extremes like heat, cold, wind and precipitation.

Suggestive Science

• Sensitive people are said to have a thin skin, while insensitive people are tagged with thick skin. Are you thin-skinned or thick-skinned? Do you think you deserve this label? Why or why not?

Science Stunners

• To make sure that it never gets worn out or worn through, the epidermis, or upper layer of skin, replenishes itself continuously. Skin cells are constantly lost and replaced by cells from underlying layers. In fact, you rub away about 13 pounds (5 kg) of skin each year during regular, daily activities.

• Your body sheds about 50 million dead skin cells every day. You will shed about 40 pounds (18 kg) of skin in your lifetime.

• When you are fully grown, your skin will measure about 20 square feet (1.9 m) and weigh 7 to 9 pounds (3.2 to 4.1 kg). There are about 8 miles (13 km) of blood vessels running through the average adult's skin.

• Your skin is thickest on the soles of your feet (up to 5 millimeters [.2 inches] in a person who usually walks barefooted). It is thinnest on your eyelids (less than half a millimeter [.02 inches] thick).

Plant Skin

I Spy Science

You're not the only one with skin around here. Check out that cactus on your windowsill.

Science at Work

Plants have a protective "skin" layer, too. To see how a cactus survives dry desert conditions, you will need three paper towels, a cookie sheet, two paper clips, wax paper and water.

Soak the three paper towels in water and wring them gently so they are wet but not dripping. Lay one flat on the cookie sheet. Roll another paper towel and lay it on the cookie sheet. Lay the remaining paper towel on a piece of wax paper. (Make sure the wax paper is slightly larger than the paper towel in all dimensions.) Roll the paper towel and wax paper together, and attach a paper clip to each end of the roll. Check your paper towels in 24 hours. How are they doing?

Simple Science

When you checked your paper towels, you probably found that the flat one was dry, the rolled one was dry or fairly dry, and the one rolled in wax paper was wet. A cactus is much like the paper towel that is rolled up with wax paper. It has a waxy covering that prevents the moisture underneath its "skin" from evaporating into the dry desert air. That's one reason why cacti can survive on so little water.

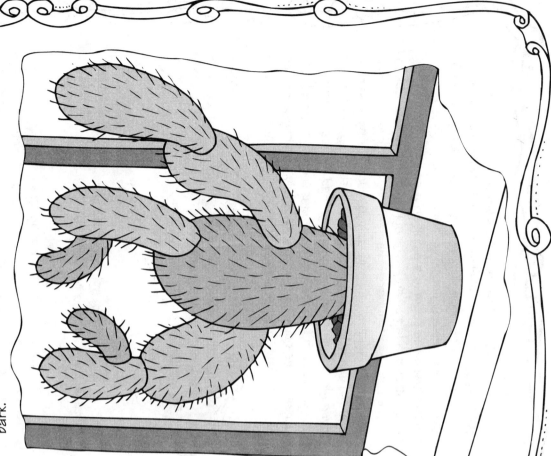

Science Stunner

• Trees have a "skin" layer, too, but we call it bark. A tree's bark surrounds its trunk and branches to keep its insides safe and moist. Trees grow upwards and outwards each year, and the new layer of wood grows right underneath the bark.

Seasonally Suitable

I Spy Science

Great! You're clean, but you're also, um . . . naked! You might want to think about getting dressed before venturing out of your bedroom.

Simple Science

Your clothing choice depends on a number of factors (not just fashion!) including weather, time of year and geographic location. Because you are a furless, warm-blooded mammal and need to keep your body at an even 98.6°F (37°C), you must dress differently for cold and hot weather. But why does the temperature fluctuate? You might think that winters are cold because the Earth is farther from the sun, and summers are warm because the Earth is closer to the sun. Not true. In fact, if you live in the Northern Hemisphere, the sun is slightly closer to you during the winter! Winter is cold because at this time of year the Earth is tilted away from the sun, and the sun's intensity is decreased. In the summer, the Earth is tilted toward the sun so the sun's heat is more intense.

Science at Work

To explore the relationship between the Earth's tilt and the sunlight we receive, you will need two flashlights and a globe. In a dark room, shine the beam of one flashlight directly at the wall. Tilt the second flashlight upward slightly and shine it at the wall. What do you see? Now shine a light directly at the middle of the globe. What happens to the light towards the top and bottom of the globe?

More Simple Science

The first light made a small bright circle, while the second light made a larger, less intense oval of light. Both flashlights put out the same amount of light and heat, but the first one concentrated the beam in a small area and the second spread it over a larger area. The sunlight the Earth receives is like the beams of light from the flashlight, straight in summer and angled in winter. Year-round, it is much warmer at the equator than it is at the north and south poles. On the curved globe, your flashlight beam spread out as it moved north and south of the equator (where the sun is directly overhead). The sun's light and heat barely touched the poles, and that's why they are always freezing cold.

Sentimental Science

- What are you wearing today? Why?

Science Stunners

- The Earth spins on its axis at a speed of about 1000 miles (1600 km) per hour and it orbits the sun at 66,000 miles (106,300 km) per hour.
- The Earth receives only one-half of a billionth of the energy radiated by the sun. Of this, half is absorbed by the Earth's surface and half is reflected back into space by land, clouds and atmospheric gases.

Short-Changed: A Morphing Story

I Spy Science

Hmmm. That sweatshirt is a little short in the arms. And what about those flood pants? What's happening? Have your clothes shrunk or are you growing?

Simple Science

As long as you are alive, you will grow and change. Looking back over the course of a long lifetime, some of this growth—like your "metamorphosis" from a child to an adult—will seem profound. But because the big changes happen so gradually, much of your day-to-day growth will slip by unnoticed.

Insects do not have the luxury of a long life, so they have to make their big changes quickly, sometimes metamorphosing directly from one form to another. For example, a caterpillar encases itself in a chrysalis and emerges as a butterfly! That would be like you climbing into bed one night as a five-year-old and climbing out the next morning as a 25-year-old.

Science at Work

To watch a worm "morph" miraculously into a beetle, you will need mealworms (available at most pet stores), a glass jar with holes punched in the lid, bran or oatmeal and an apple or potato.

Place a handful of bran or oatmeal in the jar. Drop your mealworms on top. (They will bury themselves.) Add a slice of apple or potato. (These will need to be replaced periodically when they dry out.) Put the lid on the jar. In a few days, your worms will emerge into their adult form—flour beetles! You can take the flour beetles back to the pet store.

Sentimental Science

- Have you ever been away from someone (or something, like a plant or pet) for an extended period and come back only to notice how much they have grown and changed? The difference is obvious because we're remembering the "then" and seeing the "now," but we've missed all the little daily alterations that took place during our absence. Write about a startling "that was then this is now" experience.

- List 10 major changes you have gone through since birth.

Fading Away

I Spy Science

You've found some clothes that fit (and you're looking pretty snazzy) when suddenly the familiar acrid smell of carbon reaches your nostrils. Is someone burning the toast again? Before you can decide whether to call the fire department or make a change to your breakfast menu, the bad smell has vanished. Where did it go?

Science at Work

To solve the mystery of the disappearing smell, you will need three bowls of water—one hot (not too hot to touch), one lukewarm and one cold.

Put one hand in the hot water. Put your other hand in the cold water. Leave them there for a few minutes. Now, put both hands in the lukewarm bowl. How do your hands feel?

Simple Science

Because of something called "sensory adaptation" or "habituation," the hand that was in the cold water feels the lukewarm water as hot, while the hand that was in the hot water feels the lukewarm water as cold. Whenever any one of your senses —your sense of touch, in this case—is exposed to a strong sensation for a while, your sense receptors get used to it, or adapt, and stop sending reports to your brain. That's why the first sip of soda always tastes the best and why the good smell of cookies baking that you smell so strongly when you first walk into the house fades away after a few minutes. You will only notice that just-baked smell if you go outside and come back in again, or if the sensation changes—if the cookies start to burn in the oven, for example. It is possible to trick your sense receptors, and that is what you have done in this experiment. The dramatic change gave your brain a false report: the lukewarm water felt cold to the "hot" hand and hot to the "cold" hand. People who live in places where the seasons change experience sensory adaptation in the spring and fall. Because their bodies are used to frigid winter temperatures, 60°F (16°C) in the springtime feels warm and sends them running for their shorts. In the fall, that same 60°F air feels cold—long-pants-and-jacket weather—because their bodies have adjusted to the hot summer temperatures.

Sentimental Science

• What is the worst thing you have ever had the displeasure of smelling?

Science Stunners

• The smell area inside your nose is packed with millions of microscopic smelling cells and tiny smell-detecting hairs.
• You can probably identify more than 10,000 different smells.
• You have five million "olfactory receptor" or smelling cells in your nose. A dog has more than 200 million.
• A great white shark can smell a single drop of blood in more than one million gallons (4.5 million liters) of water. That's because two-thirds of its brain is used for smelling.
• A bad smell can be a lifesaver. Because dangerous things like rotting food (or Brussels sprouts and burnt toast) give off a foul odor, your brain gets advance notice that something is wrong—and warns you to steer clear before you take a potentially deadly bite.
• When toast burns, it undergoes a chemical change. The toast's molecules are rearranged by heat and it is no longer the same substance. What is left is carbon—a completely different substance.

A Bit O' Spit

I Spy Science

Your brain probably isn't too thrilled at the thought of eating burnt toast, but if it were, it would be getting your body ready to eat by making your mouth water. When your brain recognizes good food smells, saliva (spit)—which is produced by six small glands around your face—pours into your mouth to make food soft, moist and easy to chew. And thanks to an enzyme in your saliva called amylase, you start to digest your food even before you swallow!

Science at Work

To see how your saliva aids in the digestive process, you will need four small plates, a dropper, iodine, soda crackers, pencil/paper and a watch or clock with a second hand.

Put the plates on the counter. Make labels for the plates as follows: *Not Chewed*, *Chewed 30 Seconds*, *Chewed 5 Minutes* and *Chewed 10 Minutes*. Put a cracker in the dish marked *Not Chewed*. Using the dropper, put one drop of iodine on the cracker. Timing yourself, chew another cracker for 15 seconds. (Make sure it is well moistened with your saliva.) Quickly divide the cracker mush into three parts and place one part on each of the three remaining plates. After 15 seconds, put a drop of iodine on the mush on the plate marked *Chewed 30 Seconds*. In five minutes, put a drop of iodine on the mush on the plate marked *Chewed 5 Minutes*. Five minutes later, put a drop of iodine on the mush on the last plate, marked *Chewed 10 Minutes*. What happens to the whole cracker and the cracker mush on each plate when you add iodine?

Simple Science

Iodine is a chemical that turns dark blue or even black when it comes in contact with and reacts to starch. The unchewed cracker contained starch—which is a large molecule made up of many smaller, linked sugar molecules—so it turned dark blue when it came in contact with the iodine. The cracker mush, however, did not turn dark blue. In fact, the longer the mush was on the plate (and the saliva was on the mush), the less intense the color change—until finally there was no color change at all. That's because your saliva contains special chemicals called enzymes, which speed up chemical reactions. Saliva is designed to convert starch to sugar so it can be absorbed in your intestines and used as a source of energy for your cells. But saliva takes time to act. Because only some of the starch molecules had broken down into sugar molecules after 30 seconds, the iodine still turned the cracker mush blue. After five minutes, much more of the starch had broken down, so the blue was much lighter. After 10 minutes, the cracker mush was almost all sugar. Because there was no starch left to react with the iodine, the mush did not change color.

Science Stunner

• As a grown-up, you will produce about 3 pints (1.5 liters) of saliva each day!

Mighty Mucus

I Spy Science

Depending on the amount of smoke in the air from that burnt toast, there could be more in your mouth than just saliva.

Science at Work

To find out how your mucus protects you from floating smoke and other particles, you will need cardboard, petroleum jelly and a craft stick.

Cut out a 6" x 6" (15.24 x 15.24 cm) square of white cardboard. Spread a thin layer of corn syrup on the cardboard with the craft stick. Take a good look at the surface. Leave the cardboard in an open area (where it will not be disturbed) for one week. Take another look at the petroleum jelly. What do you see?

Simple Science

The air that you breathe is not exactly clean, but it has to be before it enters your lungs. That's where mucus comes in. Your nose, throat and respiratory tract are lined with mucus—a clear, sticky liquid that traps dust and contains special chemicals to kill airborne bacteria.

When you looked at your piece of cardboard after a week, you probably noticed small particles stuck in the petroleum jelly. Without mucus and other dust traps, particles like these would find their way into your lungs. The hairs in your nose, while sometimes unsightly, have an important job. They trap large particles and are the first line of dirt defense. Then the respiratory system takes over. It is lined with special cells that produce mucus, which is sticky like the petroleum jelly. Dust particles stick to the mucus and are swept out of the respiratory system by the small hairs, called cilia, that line the cells. When you blow your nose or clear your throat and spit, you are ridding your body of dusty, dirty mucus.

Science Stunner

- Your mucus is mighty, so mighty that it can kill bacteria! It is the dead bacteria in your mucus that turns it green or yellow when you are sick.

The Nose Knows

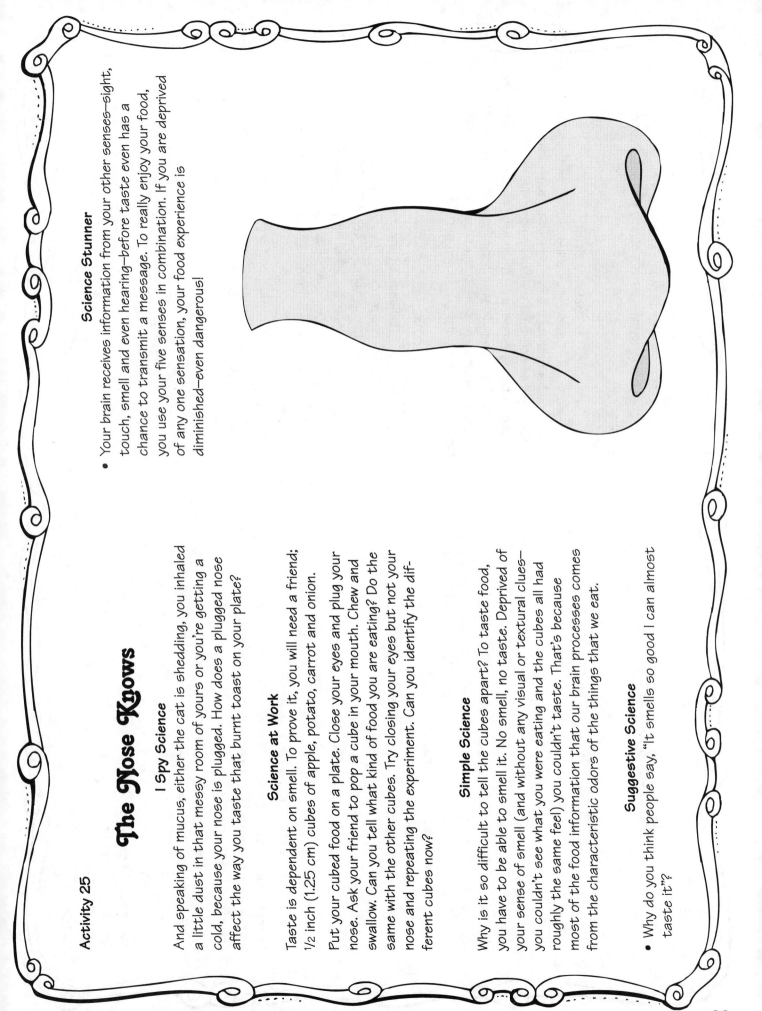

I Spy Science

And speaking of mucus, either the cat is shedding, you inhaled a little dust in that messy room of yours or you're getting a cold, because your nose is plugged. How does a plugged nose affect the way you taste that burnt toast on your plate?

Science at Work

Taste is dependent on smell. To prove it, you will need a friend; ½ inch (1.25 cm) cubes of apple, potato, carrot and onion.

Put your cubed food on a plate. Close your eyes and plug your nose. Ask your friend to pop a cube in your mouth. Chew and swallow. Can you tell what kind of food you are eating? Do the same with the other cubes. Try closing your eyes but not your nose and repeating the experiment. Can you identify the different cubes now?

Simple Science

Why is it so difficult to tell the cubes apart? To taste food, you have to be able to smell it. No smell, no taste. Deprived of your sense of smell (and without any visual or textural clues—you couldn't see what you were eating and the cubes all had roughly the same feel) you couldn't taste. That's because most of the food information that our brain processes comes from the characteristic odors of the things that we eat.

Suggestive Science

• Why do you think people say, "It smells so good I can almost taste it"?

Science Stunner

• Your brain receives information from your other senses—sight, touch, smell and even hearing—before taste even has a chance to transmit a message. To really enjoy your food, you use your five senses in combination. If you are deprived of any one sensation, your food experience is diminished—even dangerous!

Taste Buddies

I Spy Science

A few good nose blows and a few tissues later, your sense of smell is back. Great. You're all set to taste. Or are you?

Simple Science

Your nose is critical in the tasting game, but your tongue—and those tiny bumps on its surface called papillae—are indispensable. Situated on the lower edges of the papillae at the front, sides and back of your mouth are thousands of tiny taste buds. Each taste bud has as many as 150 "tasting cells" and it is these taste receptors that allow you to identify the sweet, sour, salty and bitter tastes of all food flavors. You taste sweet flavors at the tip of your tongue (there are a few salt tasters here, too), salty flavors along the front sides, sour flavors along the sides at the rear and bitter flavors way at the back. (You also have about 1000 taste buds on the top of your mouth and in your cheeks.)

Science at Work

To test your taste buds, you will need cotton swabs, water, salty water, sugary water, lemon juice and unsweetened grapefruit juice.

Dip cotton swab in one of your four taste testers. Now touch the swab to the tip of your tongue. Do you taste anything? Rinse your mouth with water. Repeat the test, but this time touch a different part of your tongue. Keep going until you have touched every part of the tongue with your taster. Repeat with fresh cotton swabs and the other taste testers. Record which tastes were tasted where on a U-shaped tongue diagram.

Sentimental Science

• Draw a tongue. Now write your favorite sweet, salty, sour and bitter foods on the correct tasty places of your tongue.

Science Stuff

• When you think of sucking on a lemon, you probably find watery saliva rushing into your mouth. That's because lemons are so sour and your brain remembers your last mouth-watering experience. When your taste buds sent the "too sour!" message to your brain, your brain told your mouth to wash away the strong taste with more saliva. Now, just thinking about a lemon sets your mouth to watering, doesn't it?

Science Stunners

• As a baby you had as many as 10,000 taste buds on your tongue! As an adult you will have about 8000, but you'll have to get by with just 5000 when you grow old.

• The tasting cells in your taste buds only live for about a week. The dead cells are replaced with new ones in less than 12 hours.

• Not everything tastes with its tongue. Flies taste their food with their feet, crayfish use their antennae and octopi let their tentacles do their tasting.

Moldy Oldies

I Spy Science

Your nose is clear, your taste buds are ready to receive and your mouth is watering at the thought of bread that is toasted to perfection. You've trashed the burnt stuff, and you're about to slip two slices of nice, fresh green bread into the toaster. Hold the phone! GREEN bread? There's something funny—I mean furry—g"r"owing on in your bread bag, buddy.

Simple Science

That green stuff on your bread is a kind of fungus called mold. Unlike most plants, fungi can't make their own food. Instead, like humans, they have to eat other plants and animals to survive. But while we eat our food first and then digest it, fungi do the opposite: they secrete enzymes to digest food and turn their future supper into mush—and then absorb the liquid nutrients. Although fungi are hard to live with, you couldn't live without them. People go to a lot of trouble and expense to stop fungi from eating your food before you do. Chemical preservatives help and so does refrigeration (fungi prefer warm temperatures), but hungry fungi eventually prevail and turn good, solid food into oozy, smelly stuff. And fungi are at the "root" of most plant diseases, digesting roots, leaves and stems. Even itchy athlete's foot is the fault of fungi. Without fungi, however, you would be up to your neck in dead plants and animals. Fungi decompose, or break down, plant and animal remains and turn them into rich compost that makes excellent soil and food for plants. And molds are used to make bread, cheese, vinegar and other foods. All that green

fur on your bread? That's the mold penicillium, from which we derive penicillin—an antibiotic that has saved more lives than any other medicine in history. And, of course, people all over the world love to load their dinner plates with a steaming pile of delicious fungi: in the form of mushrooms, that is.

Science at Work

When it's not growing on the bread you want to toast for breakfast, mold is both functional and beautiful. To design your own mold mosaic—in something other than your bread bag—you will need a plastic or aluminum container, soil, water, discarded bits of food (not meat), plastic wrap and an elastic band.

Put an inch of soil in the bottom of your container. Place your food bits—bread, orange peels, cheese (anything other than meat that you have ever seen covered in a furry, green blanket)—on top of the soil. Lightly water your mosaic and then cover it tightly with plastic wrap. Use the elastic band to hold the wrap firmly in place. Put your mosaic in a warm, dark place. Check it daily for changes. If nothing happens after a few days, add a little more water. Soon, your mold mosaic will be in full and colorful bloom.

Yeasty Beasties

I Spy Science

Speaking of bread and fungi, have you ever seen bread or pizza dough before and after it rises? How does something so small grow to be so big?

Science at Work

To see some yeasty beasties at work, you will need a spoon, a glass, flour, yeast, water and a bowl.

Scoop six large spoonfuls of flour and one large spoonful of yeast into the glass. Add water, a few drops at a time, and stir. Continue to add water until your mixture has the consistency of peanut butter. Transfer your mixture to a bowl and put it in a warm place. Check the bowl every 10 minutes to see what has happened.

Simple Science

Although it doesn't look alive, yeast is actually a living single-celled organism, and in your experiment you provided this useful fungus with the conditions it required to become active. Chemicals in the yeast started to digest the flour, converting it to carbon dioxide gas and alcohol. The flour-and-water mixture trapped the gas and began to swell, continuing to grow, or rise, as the yeast feasted.

Science Stuff

- To see how important heat is to the "rising" process above, try this. To each of two empty glasses, add 1/4 teaspoon of dry yeast and 4 teaspoons of sugar. Add 3/4 cup of cold water to one glass and 3/4 cup of warm water (not hot) to the other glass. What happens? Do the contents of the two glasses behave differently? The warm water enables the yeast to break down the sugar, giving off alcohol and carbon dioxide gas. You can see the carbon dioxide gas bubbling up in the solution. Without heat, the yeast in the cold glass could not break down the sugar.

Activity 27 continued

Science Stuff

- To put mold on hold, at least for a while, companies often put preservatives in their breads and other foods. Try growing mold on breads with and without preservatives. How long can the preservatives hold the mold? (To speed your experiment, try putting a slice of each in a plastic baggie. Moisten two paper towels and place one in each baggie. Put the bags in a warm, dark closet and check them daily.) Try different kinds of bread, like white and whole grain. Do some breads stay mold-free longer than others? And what about refrigeration? How long can you hold the mold with cold?

Sentimental Science

- What is the grossest thing you've ever found in your fridge?

Science Stunners

- With more than 100,000 different types—including food mold, yeast and mushrooms—fungi are the most numerous plants in the world.
- A small garden contains at least 10 times as many fungi in its soil as there are people on Earth!
- Vinegar is made when beverages such as wine, cider and malt liquor ferment. Fermentation is the breakdown of plant material by yeast or bacteria. It is the acetic acid in vinegar that gives it its distinctive sour flavor.

The (Empty/Full) Cereal Box Paradox

I Spy Science

Okay. Toast is out. Fungus is definitely not on the breakfast menu. What about some cereal, instead? Great. You can get your tongue around that. Just grab that box over . . . GASP! It's empty! Or is it?

Science at Work

The cereal might be gone, but the box is not empty. In fact, it's full–of air! Even though we can't see it, air is all around us. To prove the "air is everywhere" theory, you will need an empty plastic soda bottle and a balloon.

Put the deflated balloon inside the soda bottle, but don't let it go. Instead, stretch the balloon opening over the neck of the bottle. Now, put your lips on the balloon and try to blow it up. (Don't blow too hard; you could hurt your ears.) Can you do it?

That's because the bottle is already full of air. There is no room for the balloon to expand. The air trapped inside the bottle makes it impossible to blow up the balloon.

Simple Science

Even though the bottle looks empty, it isn't. It's completely full of air molecules that are floating around and bumping into one another and creating pressure. There just isn't any room left for the balloon.

Science Stuff

• Try this cool science trick on a friend. Stuff a paper towel into the bottom of an empty drinking glass. Tell your friend that you can completely submerge the glass in a bowl of water without wetting the paper towel. Turn the glass upside down (make sure the paper towel doesn't fall out!) and push it straight down into the water. (Keep the mouth of the glass horizontally; don't tip it.) Hold the glass under-water for as long as you want; then carefully pull it up and remove the dry paper towel. Is your friend amazed? It was nothing–literally! Even though your glass looked empty, it was full of air; there was no room for the water, and the air couldn't escape from the glass because it is lighter than the water.

Sentimental Science

• Is your glass half empty or half full? An optimist is some-one who looks at things in a positive way. A pessimist is someone who adopts a more negative view. To an optimist a partial glass of water looks half full. To a pessimist, it looks half empty. (Scientists, of course, look at the glass and know that it is full–half with water, half with air! Scientists are really optimistic. They even call empty glasses full–full of air!) So which are you: an optimist or a pessimist?

• Write about a time when there was just no more room–in the car, in your backpack, in the garbage, in the movie the-ater . . . . .

Don't Judge a Banana by Its Color

This breakfast thing just isn't coming together. Is there any fruit in the house? How about one of those . . . GULP . . . black bananas. Never mind. They must be rotten. Or are they?

I Spy Science

Science at Work

To see if bananas are like books—and you know that you can't judge a book by its cover—you will need five green (unripe) bananas.

Put one banana on the counter, one in a window, one in the fridge, one in the freezer and one in the basement (or any other cool place). Check on your bananas every day. Which banana turns black first? Peel the blackened bananas and taste them. Are they still edible?

Simple Science

Contrary to what you might think, those black spots that appear on your bananas aren't bruises. All bananas turn black as they age—even ones that have never been handled or bumped. The blackening is due to the presence of a natural hormone, called ethylene, which ripens the fruit. Although you can't stop the production of ethylene, you can slow it down—by putting your bananas in a cool (but not cold!) place. As long as the banana hasn't over-ripened, even a completely black one will still taste fine under its peel.

Why did the banana you put in the fridge turn black so quickly? Bananas grow in tropical places and aren't used to the cold. When you put your banana in the fridge, the cold temperatures killed the cells on the surface of the peel, which produced another blackening compound—polyphenals.

Science Stuff

• Have you ever eaten a frozen banana? Try this the next time you want a really cool treat. Peel a banana. Push a craft stick halfway into one end of the banana. Ask an adult to melt some chocolate and dip your banana in the melted chocolate until it is completely coated. If you want, you can quickly roll your chocolate-covered banana in nuts or candy sprinkles. Cover your banana in plastic wrap and put it in the freezer. Leave it overnight. In the morning, unwrap your bananasicle and enjoy a sweet—and healthy— treat for breakfast!

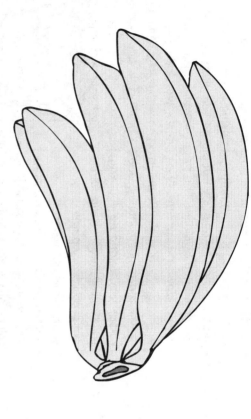

An "Egg"splosive Breakfast

I Spy Science

If you don't get something to eat in the next few minutes, you're going to go to school hungry, and that's not good. Scientists know that kids learn better on a full stomach. Hey, what about a hard-boiled egg? Now that's a great breakfast choice. Lacking only vitamin C, eggs are one of nature's most nutritionally complete and perfect foods.

Science at Work

But how can you prevent your egg from cracking open in the boiling water? To find out, you will need 4 eggs, a needle, two pots of boiling water and vinegar.

With an adult helper, place two pots of water on the stove and bring them to a boil. Take your eggs out of the fridge. While they are still cold, poke a hole in the wide end of one of the eggs. Put these eggs in one of the pots of boiling water. Add several drops of vinegar to the other pot of water. Put the remaining eggs in this pot. What happens to the eggs?

Simple Science

At the wide end of the egg, underneath the eggshell, is an air sac. This air sac expands when the egg is heated. If the air expands too quickly, the eggshell will crack with the pressure. Poking a hole in the wide end of the egg before cooking—and giving the expanding air a place to escape—is the best way to prevent your eggs from cracking. (Another way to minimize the risk of cracked shells is to heat your eggs slowly, placing them in cold water and bringing that water gradually to a gentle, rolling boil.) Putting vinegar in the water didn't stop your eggs from cracking. But it did help to reduce seepage from any cracks that occurred by coagulating (clotting or congealing) the leaking egg whites.

Science Stunners

- There are a few ways to determine the relative freshness of an egg: air trapped inside a fresh, raw egg will cause it to float in water (over time the trapped air escapes through the shell causing old eggs to sink); a fresh egg will have a very large chalazae (the thick, edible, rope-like piece of egg white that anchors the yolk in the middle of the egg); and the presence of carbon dioxide makes the egg whites of a fresh egg cloudy (this gas eventually escapes leaving the whites transparent).

- To tell a raw egg from a hard-boiled egg without cracking the shell, set the egg on a hard surface and spin it. If it spins evenly, it is hard-boiled. If it wobbles, it's raw.

Science Stuff

- Cut in half width-wise, an eggshell forms a perfect dome. See how much weight these natural superstructures can support by cutting four eggshells in half. (To prevent cracking, run a line of tape around the middle of the egg before cutting.) Place the four domes on a hard, flat surface. Start piling books on top of your four eggs. The shells can take an extraordinary amount of weight because domes are one of the strongest shapes, carrying weight down along their curved walls to their wide bases. In a dome, no one point supports the entire weight of the object on top. That's why dome shapes are often used to construct buildings that can't have pillars for support, like sports arenas.

Hot Pots

I Spy Science

Would it be more wise—time-wise and energy-wise, that is—to hard-boil your egg with the lid on or off the pot?

Science at Work

To discover the wise way to boil your egg, you will need two same-size pots with lids, water, measuring cup and a stove.

Use the measuring cup to fill both pots to roughly the halfway point. (Make sure you put the same amount of water in both pots.) With the help of an adult, preheat the burners to the same temperature. Put the lid on one pot and place the pot on one of the burners. Put the other pot, without a lid, on the remaining burner. Which pot boils first? (The water in the lidded pot has come to a boil when water vapor begins to push out from under the lid.)

Simple Science

As you bring water to a boil, some of its molecules start to move quickly. The moving molecules collide with other molecules and get them rushing around, too. When all the water molecules are bouncing and bumping into one another, the water boils.

As the water heats, however, the moving molecules at its surface escape in the form of water vapor. With no lid to trap them, these molecules disperse into the air and their energy is lost. Putting a lid on the pot traps the molecules—and their bouncing energy—forcing them to continue colliding with the water molecules. Because the lid keeps the energy inside the pot, this water boils first.

Science Stuff

• Even if you set your stove elements at different temperatures—one high and one low—your eggs would still take the same amount of time to cook in boiling water. That's because water cannot be heated above 212°F (100°C) without turning into a gas, or water vapor. The water in one pot may be bubbling like crazy while the water in the other is just gently rolling, but they are still boiling at the same temperature. All you are doing by heating the water to a furious boil is wasting energy.

Suggestive Science

Is the expression, "A watched pot never boils" scientifically accurate? What do you think is meant by this old adage? Think of a time in your life when you can relate to the sentiment behind the statement.

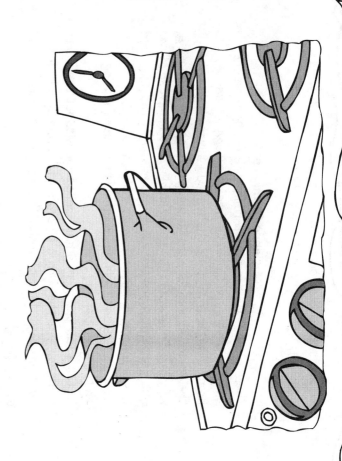

Milk Magic

I Spy Science

So you finally have something to eat–a nice hard-boiled egg. But aren't you thirsty? How about some nice, cold, fresh milk?

Simple Science

Thanks to French scientist and inventor Louis Pasteur (1822-1895), that milk–which came from a cow days ago–is still fit to drink. Louis was able to prove that certain kinds of bacteria (single-celled organisms that cannot produce their own food and can only been seen with a microscope) cause disease. To destroy the harmful bacteria in milk and beer, he invented a heating process called pasteurization. (Can you guess where the name came from?) But Louis's discovery did much more than prolong the life of dairy products–it radically improved and extended human life as well. By proving his germ theory, Louis convinced doctors and surgeons of the importance of washing their hands and sterilizing their instruments before an operation, all but putting an end to the terrible plagues that killed millions of people before the middle of the 19th century. As a result of Louis' incredible discovery, one of the greatest in medical history, life expectancy doubled and the human population exploded.

That's great, but why do we have to refrigerate pasteurized milk? Because even after heating, bacteria will eventually grow in the milk. Refrigeration slows down or inhibits the growth of bacteria and keeps our milk–and other foods–fresh longer.

Science at Work

To see how the cold–and pickling–keep bacteria at bay, you will need four glasses, four beef bouillon cubes, water, salt, vinegar and a refrigerator.

Fill the glasses with water and put a bouillon cube in each. Put three of the glasses in a sunny place. Stir a teaspoon of salt into the first glass and a teaspoon of vinegar into the second. Do nothing to the third and fourth glasses, and put the fourth glass in the fridge. Check the glasses every day for the next week and record any changes you observe.

More Simple Science

In less than a week, the untreated glass was probably colonized by millions of microscopic bacteria that turned the water cloudy. You might even have seen some mold on the surface–the green and white calling card of microscopic air-borne fungi that settled down on the water and started to grow. The bouillon provided the bacteria and mold with a fantastic habitat, so they quickly moved in and multiplied. But what about the other glasses? The vinegar and salt kill bacteria and mold, so these glasses were clear. And the glass in the refrigerator–clear, too. The cold put the mold on hold!

Science Stunners

• Scientists think that there are as many as 100 trillion bacteria living in and on the human body. Most of these bacteria live in the intestine, and we would die without them. In fact, some infections are harmful because they decrease the number of friendly bacteria living in our bodies.

• Your garbage smells because it contains rotting food–and rotting food contains bacteria. Fortunately, some of the bacteria that are breaking down your food waste give off a foul odor. That smell warns you not to eat the garbage (as if you would!), which is a good thing; eating rotten food can make you gravely ill.

• Bacteria can even be used to help sick people get well. Scientists discovered the organism that produces streptomycin, an important antibiotic, in the heavily manured soil surrounding a henhouse.

• Bacteria are amazingly resilient. Some live in boiling hot water; others survive radiation that would kill a human. Some, like those discovered living 4500 feet below the

ground, exist in total darkness feeding on nutrients they extract from rocks.

• There are more microorganisms (including bacteria) inhabiting Earth than any other living thing. Because they can tolerate such high heats (up to 230°F or 110°C) and can live in rocks at great depths, scientists think that microbes could be living in the upper three percent of the Earth's crust. If microbes inhabited just one percent of the pores in this rocky crust, and if these microbes suddenly surfaced, they could cover the entire Earth to a depth of five feet!

Energy Boosters

I Spy Science

You're dressed, your stomach is full and you're ready for school. There's just one teeny problem: flopping down on the couch for a little TV time seems a lot more "do-able" than rushing out the door for a long, hard day of learning. But while you are feeling a little lethargic–even lazy–somewhere, someone (your younger sibling, maybe?) is just bursting with excess energy. Wow. Wouldn't it be nice if that bundle of energy could transfer some extra get-up-and-go to you–because somewhere between your bedroom and the kitchen, yours seems to have got up and went!

Science at Work

To see how energy is transferred from one object to another, you will need a basketball, a tennis ball and a friend.

Ask your friend to hold the basketball in one hand and the tennis ball in the other. With his hands at the same height, ask your friend to drop the two balls. From a squatting position, watch the balls carefully. Does one bounce higher than the other? Now ask your friend to hold the basketball in one hand and balance the tennis ball on top of the basketball. Ask your friend to let go of the two balls at the same time. How high do they bounce?

Simple Science

Objects get energy from falling. The amount of energy depends on the weight of the object that is falling. Both balls have energy from falling, but because the basketball is so much

heavier, it contains much more energy. When the balls hit the ground, a lot of the energy from the basketball was transferred to the tennis ball. All that extra energy boosted the tennis ball into the air.

Suggestive Science

- "The bigger they are, the harder they fall." Have you ever noticed that little kids can take a nasty tumble and bounce back up unhurt, but the same fall can seriously injure an adult? How can you explain this phenomenon–and the old adage that goes along with it–using the Simple Science on this page?

Sentimental Science

- Wouldn't it be neat if energy could be transferred from one person to another, just like it was transferred from the basketball to the tennis ball? What would you do with an energy boost? If you could give a little of your extra energy to someone else, whom would you choose as your energy recipient? Why?

Seedy Walk Sockery

I Spy Science

You've mustered up the energy to head off for school. You'd better lace up those sneakers and get going. Since you have a few extra minutes, pull an old pair of socks over your shoes, take the long way to school and learn how plants get around without the luxury of legs.

Science at Work

Plants can't walk—or even move physically from one place to another unless we dig them up and move them—but they do get around, with and without our help. To find out how, you will need an old pair of extra-large white socks, a field or woods you can walk through, a shallow foil pan and water.

As long as it is okay with your caregiver, pull the socks over your shoes and walk through the woods or an overgrown field on your way to school. (It is best to take your sock walk in the early fall, but you can try it in spring and summer.) When your feet are covered in nature's little cling-ons, carefully remove your socks and store them in a safe place for later. When you get home, put a little water in the foil pan and add the socks. Put your sockery in a sunny spot indoors, and water it regularly to keep the socks moist (but not wet). In a matter of days, the seeds on your socks—yes, those little cling-ons were seeds!—will start to grow. Nurture your sockery for a while and see if you can identify the plants that you have transferred from the field or woods to your home.

Simple Science

Just like most human children eventually grow up and move away from home, so do most seeds. If every seedling tried to root "at home," there wouldn't be enough food, sunlight or room for healthy development. Plants can't walk, ride bikes, wheel wheelchairs or drive cars, but nature has provided them with lots of effective dispersal (or spreading out) strategies to make sure future generations get around. Look at your socks. Those burrs—seedcases which are specially designed to stick to the fur (and clothing) of passing animals—used their hooks or barbs to hitch a ride on your feet! Fruit trees use animals for dispersal, too, but in a very different way. They wrap their seeds in tasty flesh that animals just can't resist. An animal eats the fruit and carries the seeds around in its tummy while it moves from place to place. Eventually, the seeds come out—in the animal's feces—and take root far from their parent plant. Maple trees produce seeds that spin like helicopter blades, and plants that live near water often set their seeds afloat!

Sentimental Science

- If you were a seed and could hitch a ride to anywhere, where would you go? Why? How would you choose to travel: by land, by air or by water? Why?

- Plants use seed dispersal to make their presence felt elsewhere. What strategies do we humans use to make sure that people in other parts of the world know about us?

Science Stuff

- Many plants, like dandelions, use the wind to carry their fluffy "babies" away, sometimes over great distances. To trap some airborne travellers, punch a hole in one corner of a piece of cardboard that is at least 12" x 12" (30 x 30 cm). Tie a string through the hole and hang the cardboard in a windy spot. Spread a vegetable oil or petroleum jelly on both sides of the cardboard and let your seed trap blow around for an hour or more. What did you catch?

Science Stunner

- Some baby spiders use the wind to get around, too. Hanging from a tiny, silken thread, these spider gliders allow themselves to be blown from place to place, often flying as high as airplanes! These airborne arachnids have even been known to blow from one continent to another!

Train Your Brain

I Spy Science

Now that you are finally at school, it's time to start using that fabulous brain of yours for something other than sleeping, eating, drinking and otherwise living—learning. And the first lesson for the day is . . . your fabulous brain!

Simple Science

You have only one brain, but that one brain is divided into two separate, joined halves. Although both halves of your brain may look the same, the two sides perform very different functions. The left side of your brain is pretty serious. Responsible for logic and reasoning, your left brain deals with stuff like math, science, problem solving, handwriting and speech. The right side of your brain is a lot more fun. Creative and artistic, your right brain allows you to use your imagination, experience emotions, develop ideas, recognize patterns, color pictures and sing songs.

Left brain and right brain notwithstanding, your brain can be roughly divided into three sections. The different parts of your brain have different jobs. The outer covering of the brain – the large, wrinkly part at the top (the "gray matter")–is called the cerebral cortex. The cerebral cortex is responsible for thinking, remembering, decision making and sensory awareness. The middle part of your brain, appropriately called the midbrain, allows you to experience emotions and certain behaviors. The cerebellum is located in the hindbrain (at the back of your brain near the bottom). It allows you to coordinate your movements so that you can get around smoothly and effortlessly, and make unconscious actions like regaining your balance.

Your brain stem is also in the hindbrain. It connects to the spinal cord (the body's main nerve), which is at the very bottom of your brain and controls your basic bodily functions and inner workings, including heartbeat, circulation, respiration and digestion.

Activity 36 continued

Your brain does not have a memory center. Instead, several parts of the brain cooperate to warehouse and spread memories. Memory is a two-step process that involves storage (remembering information) and retrieval (finding stored information). We all have short-term memories—ones that fade quickly—and long-term memories—ones that last a lifetime. You can practice your memorization skills and improve your ability to store information in your long-term memory bank, just like you can practice your basketball skills and improve your ability to shoot successfully from the three-point line. The more you try to remember things, the better you will get at it.

rize the order of the colors of the rainbow for a science test you can make a name, ROY G. BIV. It isn't a real person, but the name is easy to remember: Recalling each color—red, orange, yellow, green, blue, indigo and violet—is much easier with the letter cues. All music students know that Every Good Boy Deserves Fudge (the ascending lines of the staff in the treble clef) and FACE (the spaces between the lines). And geography students Never Eat Shredded Wheat (N,E,S,W) when recalling the points of the compass.

To try this out, ask a friend to put 10 or 15 objects in a line. Study the objects for 30 seconds. Now close your eyes and try to remember all 10 or 15 objects in order. Can you do it? This time, make up a silly acronym or sentence using the first letter of the word for each object. Close your eyes and test your memory again. Did the memory trick help?

Science at Work

There are a few memory tricks you can use to aid your powers of recall. Try using some of these the next time you have to study for a test!

Mental Word Picture Lists

Ask a friend to write down a list of 20 unrelated objects. (In studying, these could be 20 key facts you need to remember.) Close your eyes. Have your friend read the list slowly. As he or she speaks each word, develop a mental image to go along with it. Link each new word picture to the previous word picture until you have a kind of silly picture story. Write down/draw your picture word list. Say the story out loud as you conjure up each mental word picture.

Silly Acronyms/Sentences

If you have to remember something in a particular order, it sometimes helps to make a word or silly sentence using the first letter from each word. For example, if you have to memo-

Point Form Notation

Writing things down—even using one-word clues—is another great way to make long-term memories. People who write in diaries can read their short notes years later and have detailed memories of a particular event come flooding back. "Had lunch with Grandma today, squeezed cheese and licked pickle sandwiches." Wow! Does that bring back memories of Grandma's little apartment kitchen, the feel of her paper-thin silky-soft skin, the way she held the knife when she sliced the gherkins, the way she let the juice drain away on a folded white paper towel, the exact place where her toaster oven sat on the counter, the romance novel she was reading at the time . . . I could go on and on.

Storytelling

One of the best ways to remember things is to tell someone —even your hamster—what it is you need to recall. Just saying the words out loud helps to inscribe them in your long-term

TLC10301 Copyright © Teaching & Learning Company, Carthage, IL 62321-0010

Activity 36 continued

memory. The more times you say the things you need to remember, the greater your chances of remembering them—today, tomorrow and when you're 100! Storytellers never forget their stories, because they have told them so many times. But when first memorizing a tale, storytellers break the story down into its main parts, make mental links between the parts to make sure to include them all—and repeat the story over and over again until they don't have to think about what they are saying. Then they start adding details slowly, and repeat the rich version over and over again, telling the whole, wonderful story to her mothers, to their best friends, to their pet parakeets, to their mirrors, to anyone who will listen.

Simple Science

You also use your memory when you learn a new task, like multiplying 9 times 9 or riding a bicycle. To learn any new task well, you have to practice. Practice—or repetition—is at the heart of all memory tricks. The brain needs time to store information about a new task in a permanent way. This is called "consolidation time." When you first learn that 9 times 9 equals 81 or how to keep your balance while pedalling and steering your bike, this information is stored, temporarily, as an electrical code in the brain. Without practice, this unstable electrical code is soon lost. With practice, however—and lots of it—this short-term or temporary electrical code is changed and stored as a more permanent, stable, chemical code, or long-term memory.

Science Stunners

- The average human brain weighs around 3 pounds (1.4 kg).
- If you ironed your cerebral cortex (the wrinkly, thinking part of your brain) flat, it would be bigger than a large pillowcase.

- The left and right sides of the brain are connected by a bundle of nerve fibers known as the "corpus callosum." The corpus callosum is about one inch (2.5 cm) across and contains about 250 million nerve fibers.
- Men have slightly larger brains than women, but not because they are smarter. In fact, brain size has nothing to do with intelligence. You can have a small brain and be very bright or a large brain and be quite dull. Men have larger brains because they have larger bodies.
- Scientists have recently discovered that women use both sides of their brain at the same time, while men use only one.

Suggestive Science

- Have you ever heard the expression, "keep your head up" or "hold your head high"? It's tougher than you might think. Your head accounts for about 7.5% of your body weight. That means that a 100-pound (45 kg) kid is holding up a 7½-pound (3.4 kg) head! No wonder your head is so heavy—it contains 22 bones: 8 in the cranium (which protects the brain) and 14 in the face. In what kind of a situation might someone tell you to "keep your head up"? Have you ever had to struggle to "hold your head high"?

Sentimental Science

- Sometimes we classify people according to the way they use their brains. Are you a right brain thinker or a left brain thinker? Why?
- Write a detailed account of an event that you don't ever want to forget. Use some store-and-recall tricks to help you save it in your long-term memory.

Eye Spy

I Spy Science

Your brain is engaged and you're ready to learn. Will you start with reading, writing or arithmetic? Whatever the subject, your eyes (and, of course, your brain) will probably get a good workout.

Simple Science

The inside of your eye is very sensitive, and too much light can damage it. In the dark, the pupil—which is the hole through which light enters the eye—dilates (widens) to allow more light into the eye. In bright light, the pupil contracts (narrows) to keep light out and prevent injury to the eye. This dilation and contraction are controlled by the colored ring of muscle around the pupil—the iris—which changes size according to light conditions.

Simple Science

The diagram (shown on this page) shows a cutaway of your eyeball (which, by the way is nestled snugly inside your head and attached by six small muscles to a bowl of the skull bone called the socket or orbit). Light enters your eye through the clear, dome-shaped cornea on the surface of the eyeball, which partly bends or "focuses" them, and passes through the pupil (the circular, black hole in the center of the iris). The lens further bends the light rays to focus whatever it is that you are looking at, and projects a sharp, clear upside-down image onto the back of your eyeball, which is lined by the retina. The retina is a thin sheet of 130 million light-sensitive rod and cone cells. These cells receive the light rays and change them into nerve signals, which speed along the optic nerve to the brain, where they are sorted and analyzed.

Science Stunners

- Your eye muscles contract to refocus your eyes about once every second—or 100,000 times each day. This is about the same number of muscle contractions it would take your legs to walk 50 miles (80 km).

- Your optic nerve—the nerve that connects your eyeball to your brain—is about two inches (5 cm) long. It contains about 1,200,000 nerve fibers.

- Eight percent of boys suffer from color blindness, or "color vision deficiency," as opposed to less than half of 1% of girls. Difficulty determining the various colors and shades in the red-green spectrum is the most common color vision deficiency.

Science at Work

To see how your eye adjusts to changing light conditions, you will need a mirror and a lighted room.

Cover one open eye with your hand. Look in the mirror and quickly remove your hand. What happens to the pupil (the dark spot in the center of your eye) of the covered eye when it is exposed to the light? (Try this experiment in rooms with different light conditions.)

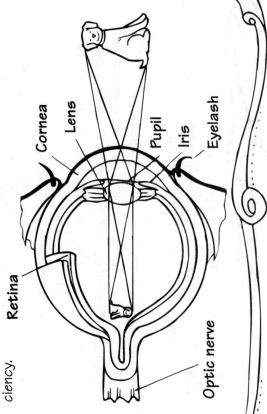

Cornea
Lens
Pupil
Iris
Eyelash
Retina
Optic nerve

Activity 37 continued

- Almost half of what you know and remember made its way into your brain by way of your eyes!
- Your eyelashes help to keep dust and bacteria away from the sensitive surface of your eye, but what they miss is washed away by fluid (from the tear duct situated in the inside corner of the eye) each time you blink.
- An eagle has such keen eyesight that it can spot a rabbit in the grass from three miles (5 km) away!
- A cat's night vision is five times better than yours. This is because cats have a reflective "mirror" at the back of the eye, called the tapetum, which gives the retina a second chance at detecting light rays. It also makes the cat's eyes glow in the dark.

Science Stuff

- Did you know that people are right-eyed or left-eyed, just like they are right-handed or left-handed? To see if you are left- or right-eye dominant, make a triangle shape with the index fingers and thumbs of your two hands. Hold your finger triangle out in front of you at eye level. With both eyes open, center a distant object in the middle of your triangle. Close your left eye. Does the object stay in the middle of the triangle? Try your right eye. When your dominant eye—the one that is favored and usually sees objects slightly better than the non-dominant eye—is open, the object will stay in the middle of the triangle. When your non-dominant eye is open, the object will move outside of the triangle. Although eye dominance doesn't have much effect on everyday life, it does affect how people play sports! Because we turn our heads slightly to give our dominant eye a better view, right-eye-dominant people might make better left-hand turns because their heads turn to the left naturally for a better view!

Suggestive Science

- Poets have long been captivated by the eyes. Why do you think this is?
- There is a multitude of popular eye-focused expressions: beauty is in the eye of the beholder; you are a sight for sore eyes; an eye for an eye, a tooth for a tooth; the eyes are the mirrors of the soul; in my mind's eye; snake eyes. What is the meaning behind these sentiments? (Choose one and explain.)
- Can you add to this list? (If you can't think of a familiar expression, make one up. Perhaps your expression might one day form a part of the common vernacular.)

Perception Deception

I Spy Science

But what if you had the use of only one eye? Would that affect your ability to do your schoolwork?

Science at Work

Activities that require depth perception–like writing, stacking blocks, pouring liquids or drawing pictures–would be more difficult to complete, at least at first. (Try each of these to see just how difficult!) To find out why, you will need: A marker, a piece of paper, a flat surface, five pennies and a friend.

With a marker, draw a target on a piece of paper. Assign a point value to each of the concentric rings on your target. Place the target in the middle of a cleared table. Give the five pennies to your friend. Ask your friend to stand at the side of the table, slightly forward of the target with his or her arm outstretched and one penny between his thumb and forefinger. From your position at the head of the table, take three large backward steps. Cover one eye and tell your friend how to move his or her arm until you think that the penny is directly over the bull's-eye. Ask your friend to drop the penny. Where does it land on the target? Repeat this exercise with the other four pennies. Make sure your friend keeps track of your score. (Does your ability to hit the bull's-eye improve with practice?) Now change positions. Whose score is highest, and more importantly, why was it so difficult to hit the bull's-eye initially?

Simple Science

Your eyes are set apart from each other for a very good reason: to give your brain two slightly different views of the same picture. By comparing the images it receives from both eyes, your brain is able to create a three-dimensional picture which has depth and helps you judge distances. When you covered one eye in the bull's-eye experiment, you lost your stereoscopic vision and your depth perception. Looking at the target in only two dimensions was like looking at a photograph: without depth (you couldn't really tell where your friend was in relation to the table), it was very difficult to judge distance. Fortunately, you would still be able to judge depth if you lost the sight in one of your eyes. You would just use other visual clues–like size, brightness and the position of familiar objects–to help your brain. You can even improve your ability to perceive depth with one eye–as you found out when you practiced the bull's-eye game.

Science Stuff

- Take a piece of cardboard and fold it down the middle. Set the cardboard on its end on a cleared, flat surface so that the creased edge is facing you. Cover one eye and stare at the crease. Describe what you see. Because you have one eye covered–and because the cardboard is in an open place with nothing around it for visual reference–your brain cannot decide which way the paper is folded. Confused, your brain keeps switching back and forth between the two ways it "sees" the cardboard.

Blind . . . as a Bat?

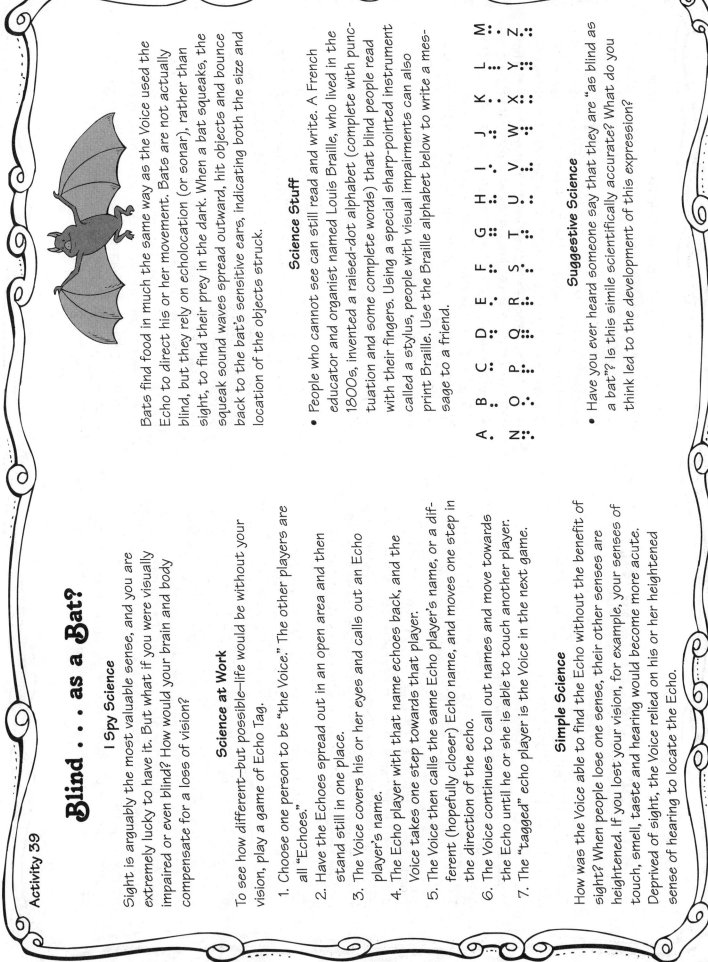

I Spy Science

Sight is arguably the most valuable sense, and you are extremely lucky to have it. But what if you were visually impaired or even blind? How would your brain and body compensate for a loss of vision?

Science at Work

To see how different—but possible—life would be without your vision, play a game of Echo Tag.

1. Choose one person to be "the Voice." The other players are all "Echoes."
2. Have the Echoes spread out in an open area and then stand still in one place.
3. The Voice covers his or her eyes and calls out an Echo player's name.
4. The Echo player with that name echoes back, and the Voice takes one step towards that player.
5. The Voice then calls the same Echo player's name, or a different (hopefully closer) Echo name, and moves one step in the direction of the echo.
6. The Voice continues to call out names and move towards the Echo until he or she is able to touch another player.
7. The "tagged" echo player is the Voice in the next game.

Simple Science

How was the Voice able to find the Echo without the benefit of sight? When people lose one sense, their other senses are heightened. If you lost your vision, for example, your senses of touch, smell, taste and hearing would become more acute. Deprived of sight, the Voice relied on his or her heightened sense of hearing to locate the Echo.

Bats find food in much the same way as the Voice used the Echo to direct his or her movement. Bats are not actually blind, but they rely on echolocation (or sonar), rather than sight, to find their prey in the dark. When a bat squeaks, the squeak sound waves spread outward, hit objects and bounce back to the bat's sensitive ears, indicating both the size and location of the objects struck.

Science Stuff

- People who cannot see can still read and write. A French educator and organist named Louis Braille, who lived in the 1800s, invented a raised-dot alphabet (complete with punctuation and some complete words) that blind people read with their fingers. Using a special sharp-pointed instrument called a stylus, people with visual impairments can also print Braille. Use the Braille alphabet below to write a message to a friend.

A ⠁ B ⠃ C ⠉ D ⠙ E ⠑ F ⠋ G ⠛ H ⠓ I ⠊ J ⠚ K ⠅ L ⠇ M ⠍

N ⠝ O ⠕ P ⠏ Q ⠟ R ⠗ S ⠎ T ⠞ U ⠥ V ⠧ W ⠺ X ⠭ Y ⠽ Z ⠵

Suggestive Science

- Have you ever heard someone say that they are "as blind as a bat"? Is this simile scientifically accurate? What do you think led to the development of this expression?

Do Mine Eyes Deceive Me?

I Spy Science

Although your eyes are awesome, it is possible to play tricks on them—or rather, to use your eyes to deceive your brain.

Science at Work

Is your brain fooled by these four optical illusions?

1. The Baffling Box

Draw a three-dimensional box. Where is the box top? If you refocus or close and open your eyes again (or look at the box with one eye closed), does the top of the box appear in a different place? Although the drawing in The Baffling Box doesn't change, your brain can process the same visual information in several different ways. The result: sometimes the box appears to be sitting on its bottom (i), sometimes it seems to be sitting on its side (ii).

2. Tricky Tops

Cut two circles about three inches (7.5 cm) across from a piece of cardboard. On the first circle, start at the center and draw a spiral outward in dark marker. Divide the second circle roughly into seven triangular sections. Color the sections in order as follows: red, orange, yellow, green, blue, indigo and violet (the colors of the rainbow). Push a toothpick through the center of each circle. Spin the circles like tops. What do you see? When you spin the spiral circle in one direction the line appears to swirl inwards and disappear into the toothpick. When you spin it in the other direction, the line seems to spiral off the edge of the cardboard. When you spin the colored circle, the colors blend together to form white or whitish-gray.

(This is because white light is made up of many different colors of light—the colors of the rainbow or the color "spectrum.")

3. Curious Curves

Use two different sized jar lids to draw two circles, one inside another. Cut out the larger circle. Fold the circle in half and cut along the crease. Now, cut along the inner circle line. Put the two pieces on top of one another and trim, if necessary, to make them the exact same length. Set your "c"s on the table so that the back of one "c" sits in the bowl of the other, with about ¼ inch (.6 cm) between the two. Do the two "c"s look to be the same size?

4. Lying Lines

Draw two vertical lines of the same length, side by side. On the first line, attach an inverted "v" to the top and a "v" to the bottom. On the second line, attach a "v" to the top and an inverted "v" to the bottom. Not including the arrow segments, do the lines appear to be the same length?

Simple Science

Your brain has learned, and follows, the rules of "seeing." An optical illusion occurs when a picture or image breaks those rules and tricks your brain into forming a false impression: your brain is fooled into "seeing" something that isn't there. Optical illusions occur for different reasons.

In the case of The Baffling Box, your brain comes to different conclusions because it has seen boxes in both orientations before. Because you have seen boxes sitting on their bottoms and on their sides and because the drawing contains equal information for both interpretations, your brain cannot decide on one correct way to interpret the picture.

We can also make trick patterns and movements that the

Activity 40 continued

brain has never seen before, like we did in Tricky Tops. In the case of the spiral wheels, your brain tries to make sense of very confusing visual information and "sees" the lines moving into the center or off the edge of the disks. With the color wheel, we confuse the brain with speed. Because the colors in the spinning wheel are moving too fast for the brain to process individually, it blends them together.

Optical illusions also occur when your brain tries to compare separate but similar (or even identical) objects, as in Curious Curves and Lying Lines. Because the shorter, inner arc of the one "c" is positioned next to the longer, outer arc of the other "c," your brain "sees" one piece as being shorter than the other. In lying lines, the arrow segments confuse the brain: one set seems to shorten the line, the other to extend it.

Science Stuff

- "The hand is quicker than the eye." Magicians count on their ability to use sleight of hand to confuse your eye and pull off their illusions. But their tricks are more science than magic. Describe the most astonishing magic trick that you have ever seen performed. Write down the performance instructions for a simple scientific magic trick. (Can you fool your friends with your illusion?) If you can't think of your own trick, use this one.

Prest-O/Change-O: From Water to Milk

Place a glass of milk in a pitcher. Pack paper towel into the pitcher, so that it holds the glass firmly in place on the spout side of the pitcher. Fill another glass half-full with water. You are ready to perform your Prest-O/Change-O trick. Tell your friends that you can change the water in your glass into milk. Without showing the inside of the pitcher, carefully pour the water from the glass into the paper towel padding. (The paper towel will absorb the water, while still holding the milk glass in place.) Wave your magic wand and say the magic words: "Prest-O/Change-O, Satin, Silk, Turn this water into milk." Now tip the pitcher over and pour the milk into your empty water glass. "Magicnificent! Scienterrific!"

As the "scientician" in this illusion, you concealed some critical information inside the pitcher and kept it from your audience. Thus, all your friend "saw" was the water going in and the milk coming out. His or her eyes fed this information to the brain, and the brain made sense of the strange message: the water magically changed into milk. Of course, this trick was an optical illusion. Your friend's brain came to an inaccurate conclusion based on the information it received from the eyes.

Suggestive Science

- There are many old sayings regarding sight. Here are two: Seeing is believing; Believe nothing of what you hear and only half of what you see. Based on your new scientific knowledge of optical illusions, which of these two sayings do you think is more accurate? Why?
- Can you think of any other "sight" adages, similes or metaphors?

True Colors

I Spy Science

While using your eyes to deceive your brain (see Tricky Tops in the previous activity), you discovered that white is made up of all the colors of the rainbow. So what makes black?

Science at Work

To find out what colors are in black, you will need a 2" (5 cm) strip of paper towel, a glass, a pencil, a black felt-tipped marker, tape and rubbing alcohol.

Tape the paper towel strip to the pencil. Set the pencil on the rim of the glass so the paper towel dangles into the glass, just touching the bottom. (Trim if necessary.) Use the black marker to draw a thick horizontal line on the paper towel 1½" (3.75 cm) from the bottom. Carefully pour about 1" (2.5 cm) of rubbing alcohol down the inside of the glass. (Make sure that the rubbing alcohol does not touch the marker line.) Check your experiment after about an hour. Is black the only color visible on the paper towel?

Simple Science

The black ink in the marker is actually a combination of colors. The paper towel absorbed the alcohol, and as the alcohol spread upward (see capillary action, page 93), some of the ink went with it. The different colors travelled different distances, so they appear in layers above the black line.

Science Stunners

- When you shine a light at something black, none of the light is reflected back; it is all absorbed. When you shine a light at something white, on the other hand, the light is reflected back.

- When dark colors (like black) absorb light, they change the absorbed light to heat. That's why dark things—like asphalt—get so hot in the sun. By contrast, light colors (like white) act like reflectors and bounce light off. They do not get hot (or at least not as hot). That's why it's "cool" (and scientifically sensible) to wear light, heat-reflecting colors on sunny summer days.

- We "see" the colors that are not absorbed by (the atoms in) an object.

Suggestive Science

- Have you ever felt pressure to do something that you didn't really want to do, or to act like someone you're not? If so, did you bend under the pressure and act falsely, or did you let your "true colors" shine through? Describe your experience.

- What are your true colors? List five of your key personality traits and assign them each a color.

Orange / Red / Purple / Blue / Green / Yellow

Activity 42

Body Talk

I Spy Science

Your teacher is asking you a question and, oddly enough, she knows that you know (or think you know) the answer even before you open your mouth to speak. How? Is she clairvoyant?

Your teacher is not a psychic. She knows what you are thinking by reading your body language, not your mind. To see how much you use your body to express yourself each day, you will need a notebook, a pen or pencil and a keen sense of observation.

Keep track of the body language that you use during the day. Describe every gesture that you make–with your hands, eyes, mouth, head, shoulders, legs, feet–and write down exactly what each one means. On a separate page, record some of the body language that you see other people using. Can you interpret their gestures? Are there similarities between your body language and that of others, or do you use your body to express yourself in a completely different way?

Simple Science

The majority of our communication is nonverbal, which means we say more with our bodies than we do with our words. People do not have to speak to make their needs and wishes known. If you met someone from another country, the two of you could still communicate, even if you could not initially make sense of each other's language. If you have a dog or cat at home, you know this to be true. Your pets can clearly indicate their feelings and their desires even though they cannot

"speak" with words. In many cases–when we are "speechless," for example, or overwhelmed with emotion–it is our silence that says the most.

Sentimental Science

- List at least five things you can communicate to another person without using words. How do you do it? Are there any "universal" gestures; actions that people all over the world use to express the same need or emotion?
- What are some common animal signals that you have learned–or been taught to–recognize?
- "Actions speak louder than words" is an old adage. Can you explain what it means? Have your actions ever said more than your words possibly could? When?
- Have you ever been "speechless"? What put you at "a loss for words"? What body language did you use in this situation?

A Matter of Attraction

I Spy Science

Check out this body language. Make a fist. Make a quick, uppercut punching motion with that fist and smile. You've just used gesture-speak to say, "YYYES! It's recess! Time to play." You probably have a group of friends that you like to hang out with at recess. And if you look around the school yard there are probably lots of little groups just like yours, each made up of people who, for one reason or another, are attracted to one another. Why are the different groups not attracted to one another? You might think that these school yard friendships are haphazard associations, but there is a science to attraction and repulsion.

Science at Work

To learn about the opposite forces of attraction and repulsion, you will need two balloons, two pieces of string, tape, a table and your hair.

Blow up the balloons and knot the ends. Tie one piece of string to each knot. Hang the balloons from their strings and tape the strings to the edge of the table so that the balloons hang halfway between the table edge and the floor and about 1" (2.5 cm) apart from each other. How do the balloons react? Rub both balloons vigorously back and forth on your hair for a few seconds. Return them to their hanging position. Now how do the balloons react to each other? Put your hand close to one of the balloons. What happens?

Simple Science

To understand what happened to the balloons, we must first understand the science of atomic structure and electrical charge.

Atomic Structure

Atoms (there are just over 100 different kinds) are the tiny particles that make up matter—you and everything around you. You can't see atoms. In fact, they are too small even to imagine. This thin sheet of paper is more than one million atoms thick! In and around atoms, there are even smaller subatomic particles, including protons, neutrons and electrons. Protons and neutrons are contained inside the nucleus (center) of the atom. Electrons move around the nucleus. These subatomic particles are held together by electrical charges. The protons have a positive electrical charge, the electrons have a negative electrical charge and the neutrons have a neutral (no) electrical charge. "Uncharged" atoms contain an equal number of positively charged protons and negatively charged electrons, which makes them electrically neutral.

Activity 43 continued

Electrical Charge

Electrical charge is one of the fundamental properties of matter. There are two kinds of electrical charges: positive and negative. When you rub something, you either push electrons into it (which gives it an excess of electrons and a negative electrical charge) or pull electrons out of it (which creates a deficit of electrons and a positive electrical charge). And when something has an electrical charge, it is capable of exerting force, which is defined as any push or pull on an object.

So What Happened?

When you rubbed the balloons against your hair, you pushed extra electrons into them and gave them a negative electrical charge, which we call static electricity. Because the balloons had an electrical charge, they were capable of exerting an electrical force. When the two negatively charged balloons came close to each other, the electrical force acted to push them apart. This is because objects with the same charge repel each other.

But why did the balloon "stick" to your hand? When an object has an electrical charge, it not only repels things with like electrical charges, but also attracts things with opposite or neutral charges. The balloon and your hand were attracted to each other because the balloon had a negative electrical charge and your hand had a neutral electrical charge (or maybe a positive electrical charge if you gave a lot of your electrons to the balloon and were left with a surplus of protons in your body!). Objects with opposite charges attract each other. (If you find all of this confusing—and it is!—just remember this simple science rule: like charges repel, unlike charges attract.)

Science Stuff

- If you look in the mirror while you rub the balloon on your head, you might notice that some of your hair stands on end when you remove the balloon. That's because the rubbing gave your hair an electrical charge. (Remember, your hair gave some of its electrons to the balloon, which left it with more protons than electrons and thus a positive charge.) The hairs stand up because they are repelling one another.

Sentimental Science

- So what does all this science have to do with your recess buddies? Do opposites really attract? How are you like your best friend? How are the two of you different?
- Throughout your lifetime, you will feel yourself attracted (drawn) to some people and repulsed (turned off) by others. What qualities do you look for in a friend? What things make you dislike a person?

Science Stunner

- It was the Greek philosopher Democritus (460-361 B.C.) who first theorized that all matter was composed of particles so tiny that nothing smaller was conceivable. He called these particles atoms, meaning "indivisible." Democritus was way ahead of his time, and the idea wasn't taken seriously for 2000 years when English chemist John Dalton popularized the theory (Dalton's Atomic Theory) in 1808.

A Bundle of Nerves

I Spy Science

Recess is over and it's back to work. You look a little nervous. Did you forget to study for that test the teacher is handing out?

Science at Work

To test the nervous reaction of a friend, you will need a feather (or other tickly object).

Make sure that your friend does not know that you are testing his or her nervous system. Use the feather to gently brush against your friend's bare skin. How does your friend react?

Simple Science

When you touched your friend's skin with the feather, your friend's sensory nervous system fed the information into his or her central nervous system (the spinal cord and brain), which processed the information and formulated an appropriate response. The brain then sent a message via the somatic nervous system (which controls voluntary movement)—GET RID OF THE IRRITANT—to your friend's hand. Your friend then tried to flick away the feather or scratched the ticklish place. (If the feather not only tickled but startled your friend, the brain also sent a message through the autonomic sensory system, which controls involuntary actions like heartbeat.) But how does it all work?

The spinal cord (tucked safely inside the backbone) is the brain's central nerve highway. Branching out from both sides of the spinal cord (which is about 20 inches or 45 cm long in an adult) and reaching every part of the arms, body and legs are 31 pairs of peripheral nerves.

Each nerve can carry many signals at the same time, in the same way that a telephone cable can carry many different, independent conversations originating from different places. Nerves are actually bundles or networks of individual microscopic nerve cells (neurons). Most of these neurons have an octopus-like cell body with lots of short tentacles, called dendrites, and a long, thin axon—the "wire" that actually carries the signal. The tips of these tentacles do not quite touch. When a signal arrives at the end of one neuron, neurotransmitter chemicals are sprayed out and picked up by the next neuron in line, allowing nerve signals to jump the tiny gaps, or points of communication, between individual neurons (synapses) as they speed through the body.

Activity 45

A Timely Reaction

I Spy Science

Did your friend react quickly when the feather touched his or her skin? Do you think you could do better in the same situation?

Simple Science

To test your reaction time, you will need a ruler and a few friends.

Bend your arm so that your elbow is at your side and your forearm is sticking straight out. Position the ruler so that your thumb and index finger are at the 0 mark. Ask one of your friends to hold the top of the ruler at the 12 inch (30 cm) mark. Release your grip so that your finger and thumb are almost, but not quite, touching the ruler. Hold your arm steady and ask your friend to release the ruler when he or she is ready. Pinch the ruler between your thumb and index finger as it falls. Where did you pinch the ruler? Switch places until all of your friends have had a chance to take the Reaction Time Challenge. Who was the quickest to react? Who was the slowest? Can you improve your reaction time with practice?

Simple Science

The amount of time it takes for a message to travel from your brain to your muscles and cause a movement is called your "reaction time." Before your finger and thumb could close on the ruler, your brain's motor cortex (which controls movement) had to get an electrochemical message to your digits via your muscles. This transmission happens more rapidly in some people, so their reaction time is quicker, as you probably

found out when you took the Reaction Time Challenge with your friends.

Sentimental Science

• Have your quick reactions ever saved you from injury? Has reaction time ever been a little too slow to prevent an accident?

Suggestive Science

• What does it mean to feel nervous? How does this relate to body science?
• "You've got a lot of nerve." Well, you certainly have a lot of nerves and nerve cells, but what do people mean when they use that expression? Have you ever done anything that required "nerves"?
• Do you–or does anyone you know–have "nerves of steel"? What do you think this expression means?
• When someone is really jumpy or high-strung, we say he or she is a "bundle of nerves." Explain this phrase using body science.

Science Stunners

• Major league baseball players must have lightning-quick reaction times to be successful at bat. Many pitchers today can throw the ball between 90 mph (144 km/h) and 100 mph (160 km/h). At that speed, the ball takes between 0.46 and 0.41 seconds to reach the plate. A quick swing of the bat takes some 0.3 seconds. This means that the batter's brain has between 0.1 and 0.2 seconds to decide whether it likes the pitch and then to tell the muscles when, where and how to swing!

Activity 45 continued

- Your brain contains about 100 billion nerve cells, or neurons, and each one is capable of transmitting roughly 1000 nerve impulses a second!

- Different nerves send nerve signals at different speeds. Some nerve signals travel 400 feet (120 m) per second!

- Most neurons take one millisecond (.001 second) to respond to a signal. Modern computer processes operate up to one million times more quickly.

- On average, your neurons are about 10 microns in diameter. If you could place all of your neurons end to end, your brain cells would form a line about 600 miles (1000 km) long! (You have lots of other cells in your brain, too. Each neuron has 10 to 50 "glial" cells that are designed to nourish and support it.)

- Long, thin branches make connections between neurons and form an enormous nerve superhighway in your brain. You have more than 60 trillion active neural connections (or synapses) in your brain.

- Drinking alcohol does not kill brain cells directly. It does, however, prevent brain cells from communicating with one another by disconnecting them. These disconnected brain cells often end up dying.

- In addition to nerves, you also use hormones (more than 50 of them) to control your bodily functions. Specialized glands or tissues which make up the endocrine system secrete these molecules, which then travel through the body and affect other organs. Hormones often work in pairs, with each hormone having the opposite effect.

Contents Under Pressure

I Spy Science

You might feel like you are under a lot of pressure to succeed at school (and to get a good mark on the test you're about to take!). But that's not the only thing weighing you down. Did you know that you are living under a 300-mile (483-km) high blanket of air that exerts 15 pounds (6.8 kg) of pressure on every square inch of your body? So why don't you crumple under the pressure?

Simple Science

Fortunately the air inside of you is pressing outwards with the same force as the outside air is pressing in. You are not crushed because the pressures are equal: they balance out.

Science at Work

To see air pressure at work, you will need a ruler, a full sheet of newspaper and a table or countertop.

Put the ruler on the table. Allow 4" (10 cm) of the ruler to hang over the edge. Center the sheet of newspaper over the 8" (20 cm) of ruler that lies on the table. Slam your hand down on the overhanging ruler. What happens?

More Simple Science

The newspaper has a large surface area, and air is pressing down with a weight of 15 pounds per square inch on every square inch of it. The weight of the air that is pressing down on the newspaper resists the ruler's sudden movement and "glues" it in place.

Science Stuff

- You can demonstrate the effects of water pressure using a cardboard carton. Cut three holes in the carton: the first 1" (2.5 cm) from the bottom, the second 4" (10 cm) from the bottom and the third 7" (17.5 cm) from the bottom. Cover the holes with a piece of tape and fill the carton with water. (Make sure you do this experiment over a sink.) Rip off the tape. Watch the water as it squirts out the holes. The distance the water squirts depends on the height (or depth) of the water in the carton. The bottom hole produces the biggest squirt, because it has the force of all the water above it. The upper hole has very little water—and therefore pressure—above it, so its squirt is shorter. (Think of how your ears feel in a swimming pool: the deeper you dive, the greater the pressure on your eardrums.)

- The pressure that air exerts can actually crumple an aluminum can. To watch this awesome force in action, wrap some reusable adhesive around the middle of a straw. Put the straw in the can and press the adhesive around the can opening so that no air can get in or out. Put your lips around the straw and suck. What happens? The sides of the can crumple inwards because the pressure outside the can is greater than the pressure inside the can. When you sucked air up through the straw, you lowered the pressure inside the can. When the air outside the can pushed against the sides, there was not enough pressure inside the can to push back, so it crumpled.

More Science Stuff

- Cut out two 12" x 1" (30 x 2.5 cm) strips of paper. Hold the strips so that they hang down in front of your mouth with the flat sides facing each other. Blow air slowly and steadily between the strips. The strips move together instead of apart because when you blow, you push away the air between them and lower the air pressure. The air pressure on the outside of the strips is greater than the air pressure between the strips and the pieces of paper are forced together.

Tummy Talk

I Spy Science

How embarrassing! The classroom is totally quiet—so quiet that you can almost hear people concentrating on their test papers—and your stomach is growling like a grizzly bear. Why does that always happen?

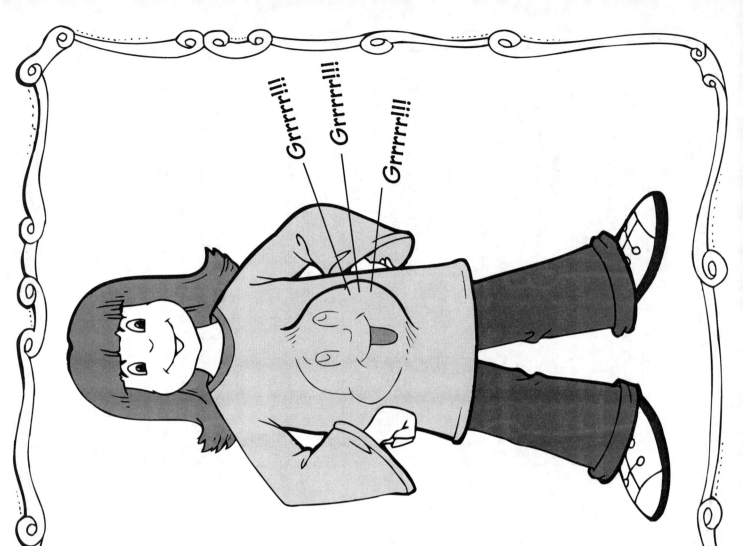

Simple Science

That growling sound is actually air rumbling around inside your stomach. Tummy rumbling—officially known as borborygmus—is a normal part of digestion. When you have a full stomach, the muscles lining your digestive tract contract in a rhythmic, wave-like motion called peristalsis. At mealtime, you might not notice your tummy rumbling as these muscular contractions push food through a special valve called the pylorus. The loud and embarrassing growl happens most often between meals when you haven't added food to your digestive tract for a few hours. This is because your stomach and intestines are always moving, even when there is no food passing through the digestive tract. When there is no mush to push around, your stomach muscles push around the air you have swallowed instead, causing the rumble. The louder the growl, the harder the muscles are working. If the noise bothers you (or the people around you who are trying to concentrate) you can try eating smaller meals more frequently to prevent your stomach from becoming empty.

Lunchtime: A Balancing Act

I Spy Science

Time to put that tummy rumble to rest. So what are you having for lunch?

Science at Work

You eat (and drink) to provide your body with the fuel it needs to keep running. When you eat right and follow a balanced diet, you help to make sure that your muscles get the energy they need to keep you moving, that your cells keep growing, that your body maintains its constant 98.6°F (37°C) temperature, and that your brain continues to function. To see if your diet is a healthy one, keep track of everything you eat over the next week. (Don't forget to include the burnt toast, egg, banana, milk or juice from this morning!—and be honest. You only cheat yourself by adding good foods or omitting unhealthy choices from your list.) At the end of each day, tally your results and compare them to the daily intake recommendations of the Food Guide Pyramid. Make a menu based on your three meals. If your diet is not nutritionally complete, suggest some dietary substitutions and deletions to balance your menu.

Fats, oils and sweets
(Eat sparingly.)

Meat, poultry, fish, dried beans, eggs and nuts
2-3 servings

Milk, yogurt, cheese
2-3 servings

Fruits
2-4 servings

Vegetables
3-5 servings

Bread, cereal, rice and pasta
6-11 servings

Science Stunner

- Your body needs:

Protein (fish, meat, dairy, nuts and beans) for cell and tissue growth and repair

Carbohydrates (starch and sugar in rice, potatoes, bread, pasta) for cell energy

Fats and oils (plant, animal and fish oils) for healthy nerves and cells and additional fuel

Vitamins (fruits and vegetables) for regulating and maintaining bodily functions

Minerals (fruits, vegetables and dairy) for bone formation and other body systems

Fiber (indigestible part of plant food, like whole grains) to keep the intestines working

Water (water, liquids and foods) for cell function and temperature control

In a typical month, you probably eat about 110 pounds (50 kilograms) of food and drink 18 gallons (50 liters) of liquid!

A Bad Case of Singultus

I Spy Science

You're in a hurry to finish your lunch and get outside, so you're gulping your food. But eating without choking is tricky when you are suddenly afflicted with a bad case of singultus—otherwise known as hiccups. What brought that on?

Simple Science

It could be that you ate too fast. Or maybe you were still upset about that test. Or perhaps there was too much spicy pepper in your sandwich. Hiccups occur when your diaphragm falls out of synchronization with your other breathing muscles. Your diaphragm is the large, flat band of muscle that lies just under your rib cage at the bottom of your chest cavity and stretches across your abdomen, from your tummy to your back. Your diaphragm pumps down and up, moving air into and out of the lungs as you inhale and exhale. If, for some reason, your diaphragm pumps too quickly and starts to contract in jerks, you have the hiccups. The hiccup sound is made when your tongue and your epiglottis (throat "lid") clamp shut, forcing air across your voice box. Anything that stretches your stomach suddenly—gulping your lunch, or swallowing too much air while crying over a test—can cause singultus. To stop your hiccups, you have to shock your diaphragm and make it stop contracting.

Science at Work

Work together with your classmates to develop a comprehensive list of hiccup remedies. Choose a remedy that you would like to try. Next time you (or someone you know) comes down with a bad case of singultus, test your remedy. Does it work? Repeat the test whenever you get the chance. If your remedy works 10 times in a row, can it be considered a cure? Compare your results with those of your classmates.

Science Stunner

- The longest case of singultus lasted for 68 years! According to Guinness World Records 2000, an Iowa man named Charles Osborne started hiccuping in 1922 and did not stop until 1990.

Activity 50

Chewed Food

because your stomach is satisfied even before you have polished off the contents of your lunch bag.

I Spy Science

Preventing a singultus attack is not the only reason to slow down and take the time to adequately chew (or masticate) your food before you swallow.

Science at Work

To find out how many times you chew before swallowing, you will need apple slice (or other hard food), pasta (or other semi-hard food) and applesauce (or other soft food).

Sample each food, one at a time. (Try to simulate a normal eating experience.) Record the number of times you chew each mouthful before swallowing. Does the number of chews vary according to the texture of the food or the size of the mouthful? Compare your results with those of your classmates.

Simple Science

There are a number of reasons why you should chew your food well (some people say as much as 17 times per mouthful) before swallowing. Safety is one. The better you chew what is in your mouth, the less likely it is that food will block your windpipe completely (and possibly fatally) during a choking episode. Adequate mastication also gives you a jump start on digestion, allowing more saliva to mix with your food while it is in your mouth and making your intestines work less vigorously to mash your stomach contents. And, believe it or not, chewing helps to prevent overeating! If you gulp your food, your stomach never has a chance to feel full before it is full. If you chew each mouthful well, however, you tend to eat less

Science Stunners

• Are you into geophagy (the habit of eating soil)? Probably not. But many animals—including humans—are. Scientists don't really understand why, but they do know that chimpanzees eat soil with clay in it when they have tummy trouble. Chickens and other birds have a good reason for eating dirt: they are toothless so they can't chew their food before swallowing. Instead, they eat dirt and tiny stones. These collect in a part of the stomach known as the gizzard. When the chicken's unchewed meal reaches the gizzard, the dirt and stones help to grind it up for easy digestion.

• Have you ever noticed that cows are almost always chewing? That's because cows are ruminants: they chew, swallow, regurgitate and chew their food a number of times. Cows eat hay, grain and grass—foods that are hard to digest. In the second part of a cow's four-part stomach, the reticulum, microorganisms break down cellulose and reform the already-been-chewed food into balls (cuds). Muscles in the reticulum send the cuds back up to the cow's mouth. The cow chews and swallows its cud until the food is ready to move through the rest of its stomach.

Suggestive Science

• Have you ever heard the phrase "chew the fat"? What does it mean? Using your new knowledge about ruminants, explain what it would mean to "chew the cud."

Activity 51

Trash Travels

I Spy Science

Chances are you missed the trash can when you tried to throw your garbage into it as you ran by on your way out of the lunchroom. This happens day after day. Why can't you hit that can?

Science at Work

To find out why your garbage apparently refused to go where it belongs, you will need a trash can and a scrunched-up ball of paper.

Walk by the trash can and drop the paper into it. No problem, right? Now try doing the same thing as you run past the can at full speed. (Don't slow down to make the drop.) A little more tricky, right? Keep trying to hit the can while you are running. Do you improve your accuracy with practice? Do you let go of the paper ball when it is directly over the can?

Simple Science

To get the paper ball in the can you have to release it from your hand before you get there. The faster you are going, the sooner you have to let go of the paper. This is because the paper is moving at the same speed that you are, and it doesn't slow down just because you let it go. Moving objects keep moving at constant speed even as gravity pulls them down to the ground. The paper does not slow down just because it is falling to Earth. The same principle applies when you are travelling in a car, and that is why the faster you are going in a car at the time of an accident, the more severe your injuries

are likely to be. If, for example, you are sitting in a car that is travelling at 60 mph (100 km/h), your body is also travelling at 60 mph (100 km/h). If that car suddenly stops (because it has hit a brick wall for example), your body keeps moving forward at 60 mph (100 km/h). (Think of the car crash test dummies you may have seen in safety advertisements, commercials or movies.)

Sentimental Science

• Now that you know about the tendency of moving objects to keep moving, why do you think it is important to wear a seat belt when you are in a car or a bike helmet when you are out riding?

Science Stunner

• In 1687, Sir Isaac Newton discovered this simple scientific law: the harder you throw something, the farther it will go before gravity forces it back down to the ground. More than 300 years later, this same principle is helping to launch footballs and satellites into the air.

Does Your Garbage Can Have a RE Cycle?

I Spy Science

Doesn't that juice bottle you are about to drop into the trash can have a little triangle on its bottom? And what about that cardboard wrapper and that plastic snack container? Those items are recyclable. Why are you throwing them away with your lunch garbage?

Simple Science

When we recycle products that are no longer useful to us, we reclaim them by using them in the manufacture of new products. This not only helps to decrease our dependence on our diminishing natural resources, but also cuts down dramatically on the amount of garbage we send to our landfill sites every year.

Science at Work

At home and at school over the next week, instead of throwing recyclable items out, put them into a garbage bag. How many bags of recyclable "garbage" did your class collect? If you salvaged this much recyclable material every week, how many trash bags could your class keep out of the local landfill site? What if the kids in every classroom in your school did the same? What if . . . ?

Science Stunners

- Every year, you throw away more than 300 pounds—or two mature trees' worth—of paper products. Recycling just one ton of paper saves 17 trees, 7000 gallons (26,500 liters) of water and enough energy to heat an average home for six months.

- We could heat one billion homes for one year with the amount of wood and paper that Americans throw away every year.

- It takes less energy to make 10 aluminum cans from recycled aluminum than it takes to make one aluminum can from aluminum ore. Almost 100% of an aluminum can can be recycled. This recycled aluminum is identical to the aluminum found in ore.

- The most common pollutant found in our rivers is motor oil which is 100% recyclable.

- If you are an average American, you throw away 4 pounds (2 kg) of garbage every day. That's 1600 pounds (730 kg) of trash every year! Multiply that by 250 million people and you get one billion pounds (one-half million tons) of garbage—every day. And much of that is recyclable.

Sentimental Science

- Make a list of at least 10 things that you threw in the garbage today. How could you cut that list in half?

Choose to Reuse

I Spy Science

A lot of the recyclables you will collect over the week can actually be reused. This means that we can use the same products in new ways instead of throwing them away or reclaiming them in the production of new materials.

Science at Work

Many artists are using recycled materials in their creations. To make a beautiful flower vase from reused materials, you will need a milk or juice carton, scissors, newspaper, water, white glue, paintbrush and poster paints (if desired).

Cut the top off the carton. Cut an interesting design along the cut edge of the carton. Rip the newspaper into strips. (You can even roll up bits of newspaper, shape them and tape them to the carton in pleasing designs.) Mix together equal parts glue and water. Dip the paintbrush into the water/glue solution and "paint" onto a small area of the carton. Press a newspaper strip onto the moistened area and apply a topcoat of water/glue solution. Continue until the entire carton (excluding the bottom) is covered. (If desired, another layer of newspaper and glue can be added for strength once the first layer has dried.) Paint your flower vase if desired. Fill with water and add flowers.

Sentimental Science

- Why do you think that some people refuse to reuse or recycle? What measures could communities take to ensure that people use garbage containers for garbage only?
- Dig up some astonishing reusing/recycling facts and make a poster to promote environmental awareness.

- Make a list of the reused materials artists use (or could use) in their creations. Use some of those materials in a masterpiece of your own.

Science Stunner

- Some artists use dryer lint to make beautiful three-dimensional pictures. (This would be a great art activity.)

The Compost Club

I Spy Science

So what about all those food scraps left over from your lunch? You can't put them in a recycling blue box, but you can recycle them. Food scraps are biodegradable. Why not start a Compost Club to beautify your school and reduce waste at the same time?

Science at Work

To find out what happens when you compost food scraps and yard wastes, you will need leaves/grass clippings and a large, clear glass jar with a lid with holes poked in the lid.

Fill the jar with leaves and grass clippings. Sprinkle with water and screw on the lid. Store your compost jar in a warm, dark place and check it every day. What happens to the leaves and grass clippings?

Simple Science

Much of our garbage is biodegradable. This means that, exposed to air and water—and with time and the assistance of microorganisms—things like food scraps can be naturally broken down into soil. This is what happened in your compost jar. Air-breathing microorganisms that eat dead things thrived in your jar. They feasted on the grass and leaves and broke them down naturally into a dark brown mixture that would normally become part of the soil.

Science Stuff

You can make a composter out of old wood and chicken wire (or even a perforated garbage can). "Feed" your composter food scraps (not meat) and yard waste. Cover your composter to keep in the heat and keep the contents moist–the decomposers that eat the waste like warm, wet conditions. "Stir" the compost once a month to circulate air and water through it. Any bad smells will quickly disappear and in a few months, your kitchen and yard waste will break down into nutrient-rich soil that you can use in your garden. If you would like to make instant compost, just put your vegetable scraps and fruit peelings in a blender until liquified. This compost can be added directly to plant soil.

Science Stunners

- On average, the garbage in a can at one home is 30% paper and cardboard, 23% kitchen waste, 10% glass, 9% metals, 5% plastics, 3% cloth, 10% dust, and 10% other garbage. That means that at least 80% of the one ton of garbage a family throws away every year is reclaimable.

- Even biodegradable things–like food scraps and paper–have to be exposed to air and water to break down. These conditions don't always exist in garbage dumps where garbage piles up. When scientists dig down into landfill sites, they find crisp lettuce and newspapers that are still legible more than half a century later!

- Plastics are not biodegradable. The plastic that is here today is here to stay. Forever. That's why it's so important for us to recycle and reuse our plastic waste.

Worm Hotel

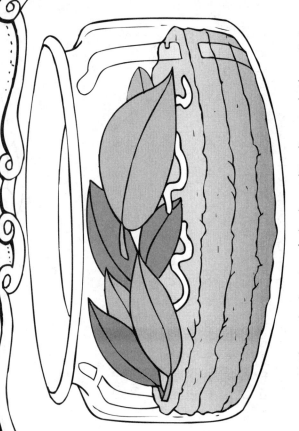

I Spy Science

There is something you can add to your school or home composter to make it even more efficient—and later to your soil to make your gardens more beautiful and productive. In Latin, we call this little pink wriggly creature, *Lumbricus terrestrus.* In English, we call it earthworm.

Science at Work

To make your very own worm hotel, you will need a large glass jar, soil, peat, sand, water, worms, dead leaves and a paper bag.

In your jar, put a layer of soil, a layer of peat and a layer of sand. Sprinkle some water in the jar until the layers are thoroughly moistened but not wet. Put a few worms on top of the sand and cover them with a blanket of dead leaves. Place the jar in a cool place, out of the sun. Put a paper bag over the jar, so oxygen—but not light—can get to the worms. Water your worm hotel regularly to keep it damp. What effect do the worms have on the soil? After you have observed the worms and their fine works for a while, make sure to put them back in your garden or composter. (If you want to take a serious crack at worm composting, you can purchase red worms and a special bin for the job. Call your local recycling association for more information.)

Simple Science

Earthworms eat dirt, ground-up minerals, organic material like fallen leaves and dead grass, and even the fungi and microorganisms (such as bacteria) that live on plants. As this food passes through the worm's body and is digested, the nutrients mix and the soil becomes loosened. Then the worm excretes or "casts." Worm castings are nutrient rich and very good for plants, which grow better in loose soil that contains lots of oxygen. That's why it is so helpful to have worms in your gardens and composters.

Sentimental Science

• Write an ode (a lofty, lyric poem that is based on emotion rather than reason and builds on a single, dignified theme) to a worm or a garden you know and love.

Science Stunners

• Earthworms are hermaphrodites, which means they are both male and female.
• Worms breathe through their skin.
• Worms can't see—they don't have eyes! They can, however, sense light with special organs on their heads and tails.
• If the last few segments of an earthworm's body are cut off, it can regenerate the bits that have been lost.

The Pulse of the Nation . . .
or Your Body

I Spy Science

Lunch is over but the games are just beginning. It's time for a little physical education, otherwise known as gym. Now that the excitement of that test this morning has passed, there's nothing like a little strenuous physical activity to get your heart racing!

Science at Work

Unless you are restricted from this type of activity, you can check your pulse at rest, after activity and at rest again. You will need a watch/clock.

First determine your pulse rate at rest. To find your pulse, put the first three fingertips of one hand on the inside of the other wrist. Press gently. You should feel the artery pulsating in the hollow next to the tendons in your wrist. Count the pulses you feel in a one-minute period. (If you have trouble finding your pulse, you can use a straw and some reusable adhesive to amplify, or enlarge, the tiny movements in your skin. Push the straw into the middle of the adhesive. Place the adhesive on your wrist where you would normally measure your pulse. The straw will move back and forth with each beat of your heart.) Now walk around the room for five minutes. Immediately afterwards, check your pulse rate again. Keep counting until your pulse rate returns to normal. How many minutes did it take? Finally, run or dance on the spot for two minutes. Check your pulse rate again and keep counting. What was your pulse rate after a short burst of strenuous activity,

and how long did it take for your heart rate to return to normal? (Try checking your pulse rate at various times throughout the day. Does it fluctuate?)

Simple Science

When your heart beats, it sends a surge of blood into your arteries. The pressure makes the artery walls, which are elastic, bulge outwards. You can feel these bulges–or pulsations –just under your skin. There is one pulsation for each beat of the heart, so when you count your pulse rate you are counting your heartbeat. When you are active (or excited), your pulse rate goes up. This is because your muscles need more oxygen. Your heart beats faster to increase your blood flow, which sends more nutrients and oxygen–and therefore energy– through your blood to your muscles. The change in your heart rate depends on the kind of activity and its duration. Heavy exercise will cause a greater increase in your pulse rate than light exercise. It will also increase the amount of blood your heart pumps with each beat (stroke volume). The time it takes for your pulse rate to return to normal after activity is called the recovery time. In general, the quicker your recovery time, the better.

Suggestive Science

- Have you ever heard a politician or media person talk about "the pulse of the nation"? Use body science to explain this expression.

Be Still, My Beating Heart

I Spy Science

Have you ever exerted yourself to the point where it feels as if you might have to catch your pounding heart as it explodes right out of your chest?

Science at Work

To find out how it would feel to hold your heart in your hands—without using a surgical instrument—you will need a balloon, a hair dryer and an adult.

Blow up the balloon until it fits neatly in your hand. Knot the end of the balloon. Ask an adult to turn the hair dryer to its lowest setting and aim it at the balloon. What happens?

Simple Science

Air expands when it is heated. The balloon throbs in your hand because some of the air inside the balloon heats up and expands. The hair dryer can't heat all of the air inside the balloon at once, however, so only the heated parts make the balloon bulge out.

Suggestive Science

- Describe a time when you held someone's heart in your hands (figuratively speaking). Some people are said to "wear their heart on their sleeve." What do you think this means?
- Would you want to take the poetic expression, "Be still, my beating heart," literally? Why not? Why do you think a poet might utter this sentiment?

Science Stunners

- Your heart is about the size of your fist. At rest, it beats about 60-80 times a minute. If you were a shrew, it would beat at least 1200 times a minute, and if you were a blue whale, it would beat less than 10 times per minute. (Because small animals move around more and use energy faster, they have small, fast-beating hearts. The opposite is true for large animals.)

- To find out how fast your heart can beat per minute, subtract your age from 220. Physical activities that push your heartbeat up to 70% of its maximum rate—and keep it there for at least 15 minutes—are heart smart. You can improve the efficiency of your heart by exercising for 20 minutes three times a week. Your at-rest pulse rate will decrease, but your stroke volume will increase, which means your heart will beat less often but pump more blood with each beat.

- Your heart can pump up to four times as much blood through your body during strenuous activity, due to the combination of increased heart rate and stroke volume.

- Blood is pumped around your body in two continuous stages. Systemic circulation pumps blood from the left side of the heart to the arteries, capillaries and veins, delivering oxygen and nutrients and picking up carbon dioxide from the cells in the body, head, arms and legs. Pulmonary circulation pumps "used" blood into the right side of the heart and on to the lungs through the pulmonary arteries to release carbon dioxide pick up a new supply of oxygen.

The Gravity Center

I Spy Science

So you're playing a game of Red Rover to limber up your muscles? Why do you automatically bend your knees and lean forward slightly when you try to break through the opposition's line or catch an opponent as he or she attempts to break through yours?

Science at Work

To learn about your center of gravity–and find out why you don't stay upright to play many sports–you will need a chair.

Sit in the chair so that your back is straight, your feet are on the floor and your shins are at a 90° angle to your thighs. Cross your arms over your chest. Try to get out of the chair without moving your legs or arms or leaning forward.

Simple Science

Everything has an imaginary spot called the center of gravity. This is the place where the effects of gravity seem to be concentrated or where the weight of an object is balanced. Your center of gravity is that point on your body where your mass can be perfectly balanced by a supporting object, such as your knees. Sitting in the chair, your center of gravity was at the base of your spine. To stand up, you would normally lean forward, shifting your center of gravity over your feet. By keeping your back straight, you prevented this weight shift. Your bottom remained firmly on the chair because your thigh muscles were not strong enough to overcome the imbalance in

your center of gravity. A low center of gravity is important in most sports–including Red Rover. Bending your knees and crouching slightly lowers your center of gravity, which makes you more stable.

Science Stuff

• To see how a change in the center of gravity affects balance, open a paper clip until you have an L shape (leave the last loop intact). Position the tip of the clip on the tip of your index finger and try to balance it there. The clip falls off. Lay a pencil on the loop and tape it in place. Try to balance the weighted clip. Does it stay on your fingertip? It does! You changed the paper clip's center of gravity–the point where the force of gravity is equal on either side–when you added weight to the loop.

Sentimental Science

• Tightrope walkers use a long pole to give them greater mass on either side of their center of gravity. With the extra mass, a slight movement to either side causes only a small shift in their center of gravity. Have you ever found yourself walking a tightrope, balanced precariously between right on one side and wrong on the other, your center of gravity shifting dangerously between the two? Describe the situation.

Silly Science Stunner

• What is the center of gravity?

The letter "V."

Gender Benders: A Matter of Gravity

I Spy Science

Why is it that girls seem to be better at certain sports than boys, and vice versa?

Science at Work

To discover the effects of gender on center of gravity, you will need a girl and a boy (both over 10 years of age) and a rolled sock.

Ask the girl to kneel on the floor with her legs together. Have her bend forward and place her arms flat on the floor in front of her, palms down, fingers extended and elbows touching her knees. Place the rolled sock at the tip of her fingers. Ask the girl to straighten up again without moving her knees and clasp her hands behind her back above the waist. Now have the girl lean forward without moving her hands, touch the sock with her nose and return to the upright kneeling position. Repeat the same steps with the boy. What happens? (Try this activity with the same boy and girl. Have your subjects jump to their feet from a kneeling position. Who has more success?)

Simple Science

You probably found that the boy lost his balance and fell forward, but the girl completed the task as specified. This is because females tend to have larger hips than males, which gives them more mass in the lower half of their bodies.

Because the point at which their mass is balanced is lower, they are said to have a lower center of gravity. (If this experiment didn't work, it could be that your subjects were slimmer or more athletic than the "norm." Repeat the experiment with a different girl and/or boy and see if this changes the result.)

Suggestive Science

- People talk about "centering" themselves, finding a point of balance, searching for stability. With your new understanding of your center of gravity, how would you interpret these expressions?

- Sometimes when we are torn between two conflicting interests and can't make a decision one way or the other, we say we are "sitting on the fence." Have you ever been in such a situation, where your center of gravity was firmly on the fence rail and not on one side or the other?

- A teeter-totter's center of gravity is right in the middle of the board, over the pivot. When you add more weight to one side than the other, you upset the balance, and someone stays up in the air. To rebalance the teeter-totter, you have to adjust the weight along the board so that the center of gravity is once again over the pivot. The easiest way to do that is to get the heavier friend to move towards the middle. We talk about the pivotal point—or turning point—of an argument or crisis. Can you think of a recent pivotal point in your life or in the lives of others somewhere in the world? What tipped the balance? Could conflict have been avoided if someone (or both sides) had moved toward the middle ground just a little?

Activity 60

Be More Flexible

I Spy Science

Did you stretch before starting your game of Red Rover? If you did, you might have been a little more flexible than your classmates.

Science at Work

To find out how flexible you are, bend at the waist and, with arms outstretched, try to touch your toes. How low can you go? To see if you can increase your flexibility with practice, repeat this stretch three times each day for two weeks, once in the morning, once at lunch and once in the evening. Make sure you hold each stretch for at least 10 seconds. (If you can reach your toes, take your flexibility one step further and try to put the palms of your hands flat on the ground beside your feet.)

Simple Science

Unless you stretch regularly, you probably couldn't touch your toes when you first tried this exercise, but your flexibility did improve over the two weeks. To work efficiently and to resist injury, your connective tissue—your muscles, tendons and ligaments—must be able to stretch. They must be flexible. Stretching before and after exercise—and stretching periodically throughout the day—keeps your connective tissue warmed up, increases the amount of oxygen and nutrients that reach and gives you a full range of motion.

Science Stunners

- At least two muscles are attached to every bone. Because muscles can only contract and relax (they cannot extend or stretch), your muscles are arranged in opposing pairs—the muscle on one side of the bone pulls the bone one way and the muscle on the other side of the bone pulls it back.
- A muscle ends in a thin, rope-like tendon, which is attached to the bone.
- There are lots of different kinds of muscles in your body: skeletal muscles help you to move; smooth muscles help you to swallow, push food along your digestive tract and operate your internal organs; and cardiac muscles allow your heart to pump. Some of your muscles are voluntary—you make them move—and others are involuntary—they move on their own.
- You have about 640 skeletal muscles, and they account for two-fifths of your body weight.
- Your biggest muscle—the gluteus maximus—is in your buttocks and upper thigh; your smallest muscle—the stapedius—is in your ear.
- You have about 40 muscles in your face. It takes more muscles to frown than it does to smile.

Suggestive Science

- Has anyone ever told you to be more flexible? Explain this using the language of body science.

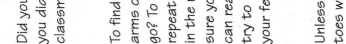

Muscle Meltdown

I Spy Science

Did your leg muscles tire during your game of Red Rover? Don't be upset if they did; it doesn't necessarily mean that you're out of shape. Even a well-toned muscle suffers from fatigue every now and then.

Science at Work

To see how easy it is to tire out a muscle, unless you are restricted from this type of activity, you will need a clock/watch with a second hand and a wall to lean against.

Stand with both feet on the ground, leaning against a wall for support. Slightly bend one knee. Raise the knee of the other leg to waist height. Lower the knee so that the foot almost touches the ground, but not quite. Raise the knee to waist height again. Repeat this action as many times as you can in 30 seconds. How many times could you perform the lift? Continue for the next 30 seconds. How many times could you perform the lift this time? Keep lifting and counting in 30-second blocks until you can no longer lift your knee to your waist. How does your leg feel? What happened to the number of repetitions you performed in each time block?

Simple Science

After you have raised and lowered your knee numerous times, your leg muscles will begin to tire, or fatigue. The number of times you can perform this activity in a set period will diminish until you can no longer continue making the motion. Fatigue occurs when a muscle loses its ability to function due to repeated contractions. When your leg muscles contracted over and over again to lift your knee to your waist and then

lower it, they used up the oxygen and nutrients available in your blood and produced carbon dioxide and other waste chemicals. That is because large quantities of lactic acid built up in your muscles and "gummed" them up. Eventually, there was too much waste and too little sustenance to keep the muscles functioning, so you had to stop the activity and let your muscles become rested and replenished.

Sentimental Science

• Have you ever felt so tired that you could no longer function, either physically or emotionally? Describe this occasion and the feelings associated with overwhelming fatigue.

Science Stunner

• The pain that you sometimes feel during or right after strenuous exercise is due to a build-up of lactic acid, which is produced by your muscle fibers when they are working. This acid must be flushed out of your system continuously or your muscles "gum up" and ache. A gentle cool down or some post-exercise stretching helps your circulatory system to flush out the lactic acid that has built up during activity, and can reduce or eliminate the soreness and stiffness you feel immediately afterward.

Don't Sweat It . . . Or Rather, Do

I Spy Science

You really worked up a lather with all that Red Rovering and knee lifting. But where does all that sweat come from and what exactly does it do for you?

Simple Science

One of the jobs of your skin is to help keep your body's internal temperature constant at 98.6°F (37°C) by sweating (when you are hot) and shivering (when you are cold). You sweat to lose excess heat and keep your body cool in hot weather and when your muscles are very active. And it's a good thing—if you didn't sweat you could become very ill and even die of heatstroke. Your body has about three million tiny sweat glands deep in the skin that pump fluid—0.5 pints (0.3 liters) in cool weather and as much as 3.5 pints (2 liters) a day in the heat of summer—to the skin's surface through tiny holes called pores. When this fluid—sweat or perspiration, which is mostly ammonia and salt—reaches the surface of your skin, it evaporates, or dries, drawing heat away from your skin and cooling your body.

Science at Work

To see how evaporation helps to cool your body, you will need a thermometer, a small piece of paper towel, a glass of water (at room temperature) and an electric fan.

Put the thermometer in front of the electric fan. Keep it there for several minutes. What happens to the temperature? Now soak the paper towel in the water and wring dry. Wrap the wet paper towel around and place the bulb of the thermometer in front of the fan again. What happens to the temperature this time?

More Simple Science

When the bulb of the thermometer was dry, the electric fan did not cause the temperature to drop. When the bulb of the thermometer was wet, however, the temperature dropped. Why? Because of the cooling effect of evaporation. The breeze from the fan caused the water to evaporate—a process that uses heat energy to turn a liquid into a gas. Whenever liquid evaporates from a surface, the surface becomes cooler because it has lost heat in the process. The fan cooled the thermometer in the same way that your body is cooled when you sweat. The reason the breeze from a fan feels cool on your skin is because it makes the moisture on the surface of your skin evaporate more quickly than it would in still air. Even on cool days, your skin is always moist. If it weren't, the fan breeze would feel no cooler than the surrounding air.

Science Stuff

- On a hot day, put a wet mitten or glove on one hand and a dry mitten or glove on the other. Sit with your hands in the sun. Do you notice a difference between your two hands? Sure. Your wet hand feels cooler because the water uses a heat from your body to evaporate.

Waste Water

I Spy Science

Do your pores only release water when you're hot and sweaty, or do they leak all the time?

Science at Work

Your skin is always losing water—even when you are not hot—as a means of eliminating waste from your body. To see this for yourself, you will need a clear plastic bag, tape and a watch/clock.

Put the bag over your hand. Seal the bag by taping it snugly around your wrist. Wait for 15 minutes. Do you see something forming inside the bag?

Simple Science

Because the water that is evaporating from your skin cannot escape into the air, it gathers as tiny droplets of condensation or water vapor on the inside of the bag.

Suggestive Science

- There are a lot of sweat expressions: "sweating it out," "no sweat," "don't sweat it," and "don't sweat the small stuff." Can you think of any others? Choose your favorite and use body science to explain its meaning. Now create a sweat expression of your own.

Science Stunners

- Why do you feel hot in 98.6°F (37°C) weather even though your body temperature is 98.6°F? Because your body is always producing heat and that heat needs to dissipate into the air around you. Unless the surrounding air is substantially cooler than your body, internal sensors warn you that it is too hot and involuntary responses, like sweating, begin.

- When you get sick with a fever, your body temperature rises. This extra heat helps to kill the germs that are making you ill. If your temperature rises above 104°F (40°C), you are at serious risk for overheating. That's why we take medicine to keep our temperature down.

- You could survive in 266°F (130°C) weather for 20 minutes if the air was dry, but in moist air you would die in that time if the thermometer rose above 120°F (49°C). Why? Because in humid conditions, the fluid doesn't evaporate. It just drips off the body with no cooling effect.

- The temperature of your body is also regulated by the widening or narrowing of the blood vessels in your skin. When you are hot and need to release heat, your blood vessels widen to increase blood flow and you look flushed. When you are cold and need to conserve heat, your blood vessels narrow and you look pale.

- Pigs can't sweat. Instead, they roll around in the mud to keep cool, keep the bugs away and prevent their skin from burning in the hot sun.

Activity 64

Not-So-Sweet Feet

I Spy Science

You understand the science behind sweating, but whoa. What makes your feet so stinky?

Science at Work

It's your sneakers that give your feet their characteristically foul odor. To find out why, you will need a jar with a lid, unflavored gelatin, water, a pot, a cotton swab and a pair of old sneakers.

Ask an adult to prepare the gelatin according to the directions on the label. Allow the gelatin to cool but not harden and then pour it into the jar. Hold the jar over the sink and tip it on its side to allow the excess to drain. Set the jar on its side on the counter. In about four hours, put on your sneakers—without socks—and run around until you are hot and sweaty. Take off your shoes and rub the cotton swab between the toes of both feet. Gently touch the swab to the surface of the gelatin in a polka-dot pattern. Wash your hands and feet in soapy water. Screw the lid on the jar and put it on its side in a warm, dark place. Check the jar in four days. What do you see?

Simple Science

Your polka dots are now indents on the surface of the gelatin. That's because microbes—microscopic organisms that live on your body and all around you—have eaten holes in their host. It is these same microbes that make your shoes smell. Your feet sweat and shed dead skin cells and microbes eat this stuff up. Your sneakers are dark, warm and damp—the perfect

environment for a hungry horde. As the microbes feast, they create waste, and that's what makes that awful smell. The gelatin jar was like your shoes: a great place for microbes to live, eat and reproduce.

Some carry disease, so don't let your experiment grow for more than four days. After making your observations, remove the lid and fill the jar with hot tap water. Let it soak until the gelatin dissolves, and then pour the contents down the drain. Wash the jar and your hands with hot soapy water.)

(Dispose of your microbes with care.

Sentimental Science

- Write a rhyming poem about your stinky feet.

Science Stunners

- The man with the biggest feet on record takes a size 29 1/2 shoe (Guinness World Records 2000).
- The most expensive shoes ever made (they were studded with pearls) were commissioned by an African emperor in 1977 for $85,000. The most expensive shoes on the market—a pair of size 5 alligator skin sandals that have diamond-studded buckles—retail for $28,800 (Guinness World Records 2000).

Shower Power

I Spy Science

You're home from school—and you're hot and sweaty. The first order of business is a nice, hot, soapy shower. The second order of business: draw a smiley face on the surface of that misty bathroom mirror!

Science at Work

To find out why the bathroom mirror fogs up when you take a shower, you will need a clean metal can, food coloring, ice cubes and a spoon.

Fill the can about two-thirds of the way with warm water. Add a few drops of food coloring to the water. Leave the can until the water inside reaches room temperature (about one hour). Drop ice cubes into the water one at a time and stir. Continue to add ice until droplets of clear water start to form on the outside of the can.

Simple Science

The air surrounding the can contained invisible water vapor. When this air touched the cold can, the water vapor cooled and condensed into liquid droplets. (We know that it was not water from the inside of the can that gathered as droplets on the outside of the can since the outside water was clear, not colored.) The point at which water vapor condenses into liquid water is called "the dew point." The bathroom mirror fogs up for the same reason. The warm, wet air moving around in your bathroom as you shower is full of water vapor. When the water vapor comes in contact with the cold mirror, it con-

denses and turns into a liquid. Many, many droplets form, covering the mirror in a thin film. When you draw your finger through the water droplet film, it breaks apart to reveal the mirror underneath.

Science Stunner

- If all of the water vapor in the atmosphere were to fall to Earth suddenly, most places on Earth would receive only about 1" (2.5 cm) of precipitation. (So how do floods occur? When air masses have a much higher than normal water content and land masses channel rainfall into specific areas.)

Activity 66

The Slippery Soap

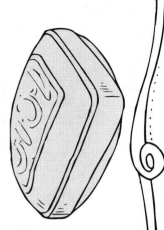

I Spy Science

That bar of soap is hard to hold on to. It keeps squirting out of your hands! What makes soap so slippery?

Simple Science

Like all things, soap is made up of millions of tiny molecules. When your bar of soap gets wet, water molecules slip inbetween the soap molecules and free them up. The soap molecules slip and slide around, on the bar and on your body. Once on your skin, the soap molecules get to work, joining with particles of dirt and sliding them right off your body, leaving you squeaky clean.

Science Stuff

- If you stay in the bathtub for a long time, your fingers and toes will get wrinkly. This is because the thin, protective coat of oil that covers your skin gets washed away, allowing the bath water to seep in. The extra water makes your skin swell and wrinkle. The wrinkles in your fingers and toes are large because the skin is thicker on the palms of your hands and the soles of your feet—so there's more skin to wrinkle.

More Science Stuff

- Your eyes sting when you get shampoo in them because the shampoo is different from your natural tears. Your eyes can tell the difference and send the "ouch" and "invader" messages to your brain. Your brain tells your eyes to make more tears to wash away the offensive liquid. "Tearless" shampoos are made to mimic the fluid in your eyes.

Silly Science Stuff

To make your own shaped hand and bath soaps, mix 2 cups (480 ml) of Ivory Snow™ detergent with 4 tablespoons (60 ml) water. Add a little food coloring and use your hands to squish the soap mixture into interesting shapes. Try pressing some of the mixture into cookie cutters or plastic food or craft molds.

Suggestive Science

- Write a slippery soap tongue twister.
- Write a descriptive poem about a few of your favorite wrinkly things.

Science Stunners

- If you decided not to wash your body, dirt and germs would build up on your skin. You would develop a bad odor and pimples. All that dirt and bacteria that you didn't wash away might even get on your food and give you food poisoning!
- Forget the soap. Some animals—like zebras, horses and elephants—roll around in the dirt to get clean! Rhinos, hippopotami, crocodiles and sharks get help from birds like oxpickers and fish-like ramoras—little helpers that make a meal out of the bugs and bacteria that live on—and even in the mouths of—their thankful hosts. Other animals, like cats and dogs, use their tongues to keep themselves clean. And apes and monkeys stay clean by getting friends and family members to pick ticks and other bugs out of their fur.

To Suds or Not to Suds

I Spy Science

Have you ever taken a shower at somebody else's house or at a hotel and found that the soap lathers better—or worse—than it does at your home? It's not the soap that makes the difference; it's the water!

Science at Work

To find out how hard and soft water affect the "latherability" of soap, you will need three same-size drinking glasses, warm water, 1 Tbsp. (15 ml) Epsom salts, 1 Tbsp. (15 ml) Arm & Hammer® washing soda (a household cleaner), 1 Tbsp. (15 ml) dishwashing liquid and a spoon.

Fill all three glasses three-quarters full with warm water. Stir the Epsom salts into one glass and the washing soda into another. Add one teaspoon of dishwashing liquid to all three glasses. Stir the contents of each glass vigorously. Do suds form in all three glasses?

Simple Science

You were able to make lots of suds in the glass with the washing soda, but very few in the glass with the Epsom salts. This is because washing soda neutralizes minerals to make water soft, while Epsom salts is a mineral that makes water hard. Soft water gets sudsy; hard water does not. Washing soda (or sodium carbonate) neutralizes water—makes it soft—by removing salts. The minerals and the soda react chemically and split into simpler molecules that form a precipitate. The precipitate is an insoluble substance that does not dissolve or mix but falls to the bottom of a solution, forms

the ring around your tub that remains when you drain your bath water. (Check your glasses after emptying them. Is there a ring around the glass that contained the Epsom salts?)

The water that comes out of your tap might contain calcium salts. If it contains a lot of salts, it is "hard," and will prevent soapsuds from forming. If your tap water is soft, it will get nice and sudsy. How did your tap water react when you stirred in the dishwashing liquid? Based on your observations, do you think your tap water is hard, soft or somewhere in-between?

Science Stuff

- You can make your own water-softening bath solution with half a cup of washing soda. Just crush the washing soda crystals into fine powder. Add them a little at a time, to a jar of water until the solution is saturated and no more will dissolve. Put the lid on the jar, and pour a little bit into the water next time you are going to have a bath. You can even add scent and coloring to your bath solution!

the air pushed with enough force to raise the coin. The expanding air escaped from the bottle in little gusts, raising and lowering the quarter as it did so.

Suggestive Science

• In science, heat always flows from the warmer outside to the colder inside. If your parent or guardian gives you the cold shoulder over this test business—fails to respond warmly to you or even ignores you—what can you do to thaw his or her frosty heart?

Warming Up the Cold Shoulder

I Spy Science

Now that you are home and showered, you'd better come clean about something else—that test you took this morning. You might get angry or even the cold shoulder from your parent or guardian, but it's best to be up-front and honest about your mistakes.

Science at Work

The power to warm is at your fingertips. To see how, you will need empty plastic bottle (narrow neck, wide shoulders), a freezer and a (wet) quarter.

Put the bottle in the freezer as soon as you get home from school. Just before bed, remove the bottle from the freezer and immediately put the wet quarter over the bottle's mouth, covering it completely. Wrap both your hands tightly around the wide part of the bottle. What happens to the coin?

Simple Science

The air inside the bottle got very cold when you put it in the freezer and when you put the quarter over the mouth of the bottle, it trapped the air inside. When you put your hands on the bottle, the quarter started to bounce up and down almost immediately. That's because the air inside the bottle started to warm up as the heat from your hands (and the surrounding air) moved through the plastic. Warm air takes up more space than cold air. As the air inside the bottle warmed, it expanded and started to push up against the quarter. When the bottle could no longer contain its growing contents,

Pop Goes the Kernel

I Spy Science

How about a little after-school snack before you start studying for that make-up test? Popcorn perhaps?

Science at Work

To find out what puts the pop in popcorn, you will need a handful of popcorn kernels, a marker, a bowl and a hot air popper (or a pot or microwave-safe container).

Pick out about 20 kernels. Make sure some of the kernels are intact and some are cracked or crumpled. (If you can't find any damaged kernels, hit a few lightly with a hammer to split their shells slightly.) Mark the pointed end of the imperfect kernels with the marker. Heat the kernels in the popper and collect the popcorn in a bowl. When the popping has stopped, unplug the popper and look at the contents of the bowl. (Remember, the contents and popper are hot!) Did all the kernels pop?

Simple Science

Popcorn kernels are actually the seeds of a new corn plant. They are hard and dry on the outside, but inside they are tightly packed with soft, moist material. The moisture is sealed inside the kernel to keep the seed alive until conditions are right for growth. When you heat the kernel quickly, the moisture inside the kernel heats up, too. Eventually, it vaporizes and turns to steam. The hot, trapped steam continues to expand, increasing the pressure inside the kernel until the shell splits and the kernel bursts open with tremendous force. When the shell explodes, the material inside expands to its full size.

To pop, popcorn kernels must be reasonably intact and moist. The kernel will not pop if the shell is cracked or the moisture inside has evaporated prior to heating. The imperfect kernels in your experiment didn't pop because the steam could not build up inside them.

Suggestive Science

- Have you ever felt so angry you just wanted to burst? Have you ever needed to blow off some steam? Imagine that you are a popcorn kernel exploding. How does it feel?
- Can you pantomime a kernel of corn popping?

Science Stunners

- Popcorn has been around for centuries. It was used by the Incas as a decoration hundreds of years ago, and was introduced to the Pilgrims by Native Americans at the very first Thanksgiving dinner.
- For a popcorn kernel to pop, the temperature inside the kernel must reach at least 212°F (100°C), the boiling point of water.
- Good popcorn will grow up to 40 times its original size when popped.
- Popcorn is a wise snack choice. It is very low in calories, contains just a trace of protein and fat and is a source of dietary fiber.

Marshmallow Magic

I Spy Science

Does popping popcorn make you think of sitting around a crackling campfire? Does sitting around a crackling campfire make you think about roasting marshmallows? Does roasting marshmallows make your mouth water for a . . . roasted marshmallow?

Science at Work

To roast a magic marshmallow in your kitchen, you will need two marshmallows, a microwave-safe plate and a microwave oven.

With the help of an adult, place the marshmallow on the plate (if you want, you can paint a face on your marshmallow with a cotton swab and some food coloring) and put the plate in the microwave oven. Heat the marshmallow on high for 30 seconds. Watch through the glass to see what happens to the marshmallow as it heats. Remove the plate from the microwave oven and let the marshmallow stand for 30 seconds. When it is cool to the touch, take a bite. Does it have the same texture and consistency as an uncooked marshmallow? (To make an edible sculpture, heat another marshmallow. This time, mold the cooled marshmallow into an interesting shape. As it gets crunchy and hard, it will keep that shape. Aesthetically pleasing and delicious!)

Simple Science

The marshmallow grows when you heat it in the microwave oven for the same reason that the popcorn pops in a hot popper. A marshmallow contains a lot of air, moisture and sugar. When you heat it in the microwave, the sugar softens, the air and water expand and the marshmallow quickly swells to gigantic proportions. As soon as the microwave shuts off, the marshmallow cools and shrinks and the sugar hardens again. Because some of the marshmallow's moisture was lost in the heating process (you can see it on the plate), the marshmallow is much drier and chewier than before heating.

Crystals Rock! (or Rock Crystals)

I Spy Science

If you like the idea of making your own crystals, why not create your own rock crystal garden?

Science at Work

To grow a rock crystal garden, you will need a dish, a glass, vinegar and a handful of rocks of roughly the same size (look for rocks that contain white streaks).

Pour a little vinegar into the glass. Drop one rock into the vinegar. If the rock starts to fizz remove it from the vinegar and place it in your dish. Test all of your rocks in this way. Put only the fizzing rocks into your dish. (Put the rest of the rocks back outside.) Pour vinegar over the rocks and into the dish until just the tops of the rocks are visible above the surface. Leave your dish in a sunny place and watch what happens over the next few days.

Simple Science

As long as it contains calcium carbonate (those white streaks you were looking for), even an ordinary rock will sprout beautiful crystals. Vinegar reacts with the calcium carbonate in the rocks and starts to break it down. That's what makes the rocks fizz. As the vinegar evaporates from the dish, tiny bits of calcium carbonate are left behind, clinging to the rocks. Over time, these bits join together and build up into lumpy aragonite crystals. (If you want to keep your crystals growing, just add more vinegar to the dish.)

A Sweet Solution

I Spy Science

All this popcorn and marshmallow stuff sure makes a kid thirsty. How about a nice crystal flavor drink? Not the healthiest choice, but it will wet your whistle. Just add a little sugar to some nice, cold water and . . . Hey! What happened to the sugar?

Simple Science

The sugar didn't really disappear when you put it in the water. It dissolved, or slipped into the spaces between the water molecules. You can't see it anymore, but that doesn't mean it isn't there. You can still taste it. By dissolving one substance (sugar) completely in another (water), you created a solution. Scientists call the solid molecules that become part of the solution (in this case, the sugar crystals) a "solute" and the liquid molecules (in this case, the water) a "solvent."

Science at Work

To witness this disappearing act in slow motion, you will need: a sugar cube,* ½ tsp. (2.5 ml) granulated sugar and two glasses of warm water.

At the same time, drop the sugar cube (or ball) into one glass of water and the granulated sugar into the other glass. In which glass does the sugar dissolve faster?

*If you don't have any sugar cubes, you can make your own round version. Just put a drop of water in a granulated sugar bowl. Allow the drop to dry completely and harden. Remove it from the sugar bowl, and voila! You have a homemade sugar ball.

More Simple Science

When you put the sugar into the warm water, the crystals in both the granulated sugar and the sugar cube broke up into smaller particles, called molecules—the smallest form in which sugar can exist. (Sugar molecules are not even visible under the most powerful microscope.) For sugar to dissolve in water and form a solution, each sugar molecule must be completely surrounded by water molecules. In the glass with the granulated sugar, the sugar crystals broke down more quickly and the water molecules were able to surround (dissolve) the sugar molecules faster, because they were spread out. The sugar in the cube was pressed together, so it took longer for the water to get in between the crystals, break them apart and surround the sugar molecules.

The Return of Sugar:
A Crystal Clear Explanation

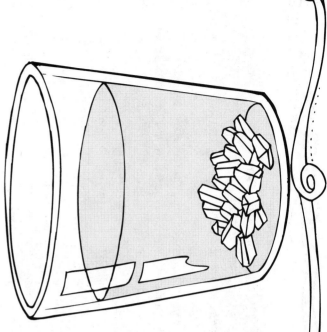

I Spy Science

In all that excitement you went a little overboard with the sugar. Now there is too much sugar in your glass to dissolve, and it's way too sweet to drink. You'll just have to dump the stuff down the drain and start over again. But wait! You might not be able to salvage your beverage, but you can make some really beautiful (and delicious) crystals with that sweet syrup.

Science at Work

To make some big, edible sugar crystals, you will need a microwave-safe glass, sugar and food coloring (optional).

Transfer your water-sugar solution to the microwave-safe glass. With an adult's help, heat the solution in the microwave oven until it boils. Use an oven mitt to remove the glass from the microwave. Continue to add sugar to the solution and stir until no more sugar will dissolve. (If you would like your crystals to look like rubies, emeralds or sapphires instead of diamonds, add some red, green or blue food coloring.) Keep the glass in a warm, dry place and check it regularly. Do not disturb the glass or its contents. What do you see?

Simple Science

As the water in the solution begins to evaporate, the sugar will reappear in the form of crystals. These sugar crystals will continue to form in your glass until all of the water evaporates. The longer you wait, the larger the crystals will be. (If a

hard skin forms on the surface of your solution, you will have to break a hole in it to allow the water to continue to evaporate.) When your crystals are fully formed, you can eat them or store them in a dry place. Use dry hands or tweezers to handle your "faux gems" and a magnifying glass for a close-up look.

How did the sugar "reappear"? Temperature plays a large role in how much sugar water can hold, and hot water can hold more than cold water. You continued to add sugar (solid molecules or solute) to the hot water (liquid molecules or solvent) until the solution was saturated and no more sugar could be dissolved. As the solution cooled, it became supersaturated; there were more sugar crystals in the water than it could possibly hold at the cooler temperature, and some of the sugar started to come out of the solution. The sugar molecules hooked together, building on one another as more and more sugar came out of the solution and formed sugar crystals.

Activity 73 continued

Science Stuff

- You can also do this disappearing and reappearing experiment with rock salt and alum (a type of mineral or chemical salt), but instead of the long sugar crystals with their flat slanted sides, you will create flat-sided salt crystal cubes or angular-sided, multifaceted alum crystals. If you would rather capture your crystals than scrape them off the sides and bottom of a glass, tie a piece of damp string around a pencil. Rub a few grains of salt or alum into the string so the crystals have something to which they can attach. Lay the pencil across the top of the glass and dangle the string in the solution. The salt crystals will "grow" on the string.

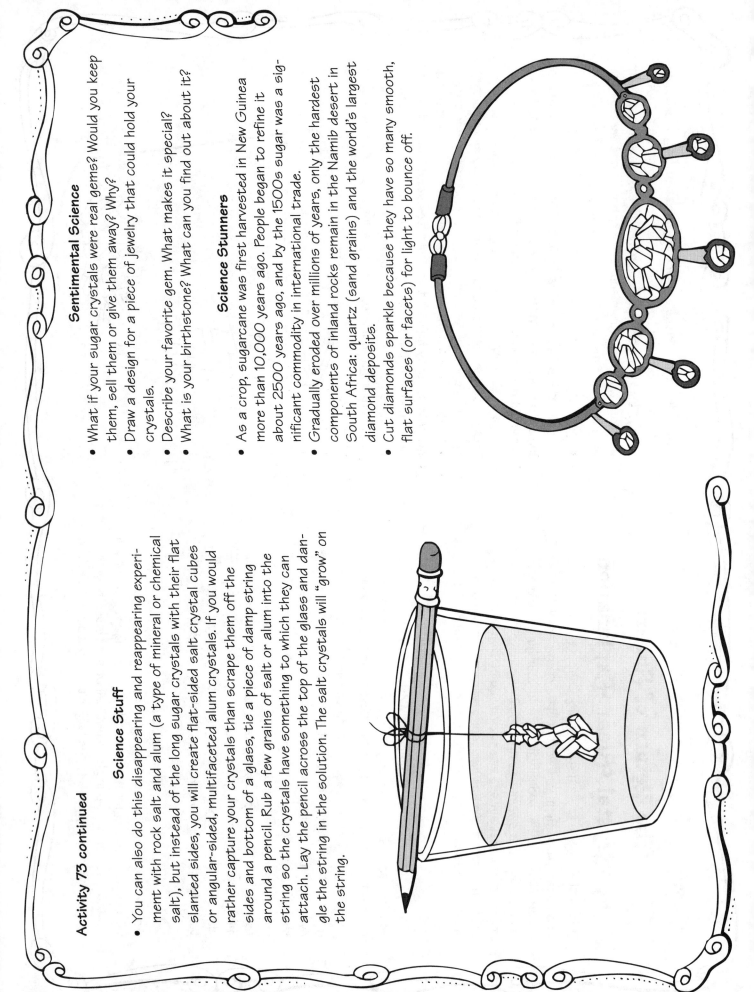

Sentimental Science

- What if your sugar crystals were real gems? Would you keep them, sell them or give them away? Why?
- Draw a design for a piece of jewelry that could hold your crystals.
- Describe your favorite gem. What makes it special?
- What is your birthstone? What can you find out about it?

Science Stunners

- As a crop, sugarcane was first harvested in New Guinea more than 10,000 years ago. People began to refine it about 2500 years ago, and by the 1500s sugar was a significant commodity in international trade.
- Gradually eroded over millions of years, only the hardest components of inland rocks remain in the Namib desert in South Africa: quartz (sand grains) and the world's largest diamond deposits.
- Cut diamonds sparkle because they have so many smooth, flat surfaces (or facets) for light to bounce off.

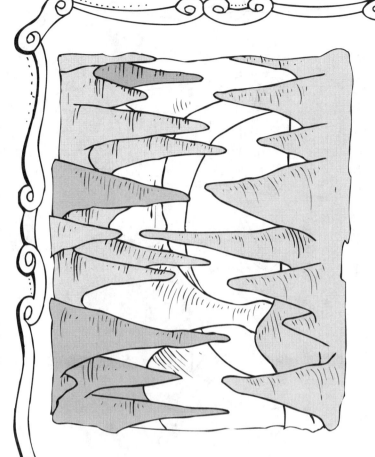

Activity 74

Cave Creations

I Spy Science

Stalactites and stalagmites are two other cool rock creations or formations. They don't have much in common with your crystal flavor drink or your rock crystals, but they can be replicated in your kitchen.

Science at Work

To make your own cave creations, you will need baking soda (or Arm & Hammer® washing soda), two tall glasses, hot water and string.

Fill the two glasses two-thirds full with hot water. Stir baking soda into each glass until no more will dissolve. When your solution is saturated, soak the string in clean water and put one end in each glass. Make sure the string droops slightly between the two glasses. Check your experiment every day for the next week or so. What happens?

Simple Science

Stalactites and stalagmites are the beautiful hard lime "icicle" deposits found in many caves. Most caves are made out of limestone which is easily dissolved by water. As rainwater seeps through the ceilings of caves, it dissolves the limestone. Stalactites hang down from cave ceilings, and stalagmites build up on cave floors as the mineral-rich water drips down, evaporates and leaves behind deposits to re-harden over a period of hundreds and even thousands of years.

The stalactites and stalagmites you created in your experiment were formed in much the same way. Capillary action (see page 93) forced the soda and water solution to travel up and across the string, where it dripped down from the loop between the two glasses. As the water evaporated, the soda was left behind. It hardened in the form of icicle-shaped mineral deposits.

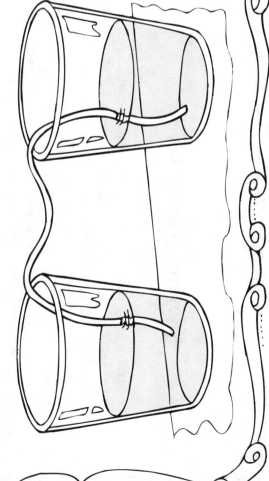

Activity 75

Moving Molecules

I Spy Science

All this crystal stuff is really neat, but what about that drink? You're still thirsty? Why don't you start over again? This time, leave the sugar until the end so you can actually see some molecules in action.

Science at Work

To get your flavor crystals moving, you will need two clear glasses, flavor crystals, hot water, cold water and a clock/watch.

Fill one glass three-quarters full with cold tap water. Sprinkle a pinch of colored flavor crystals into the glass and check the time. Watch what happens to the flavor crystals. When nothing more is happening in the glass, check the time again. How much time has elapsed? Fill the other glass with the same amount of hot tap water, and repeat the experiment. (Make sure you use the same size pinch of flavor crystals.) What happens this time?

Simple Science

Eventually, the colored flavor crystals spread evenly throughout both glasses, coloring the water evenly, but this happened much more rapidly in the glass that contained the warm water. Each drop of water is made up of millions of molecules. These molecules move constantly throughout both glasses. Heat energy causes the water molecules in the warm water to move much faster than those in the cold water, which allows the colored crystals to spread more quickly.

Science Stunners

- Most living things are at least one-half water. You are 65% water by weight. Skinny people may be as much as 75% water; heavy people as little as 55%.
- Water is the only thing on Earth that exists naturally in three states: solid (ice), liquid (water) and gas (water vapor).
- In all states, water molecules are in constant motion. When water is heated to 212°F (100°C) the molecules move fast enough to boil off as water vapor. When it is cooled below 32°F (0°C), the molecules move much more slowly and form ice.
- 70% of the Earth's surface is covered by water.
- More than 97% of all water found on Earth is salty. Only 3% is fresh water. Of that, 75% percent is frozen in the form of ice caps, glaciers and icebergs. Another 20% is underground. That means that we have access to only 5% of our total fresh water reserve, and that water is found in lakes, rivers and clouds.
- There are more molecules of water in a single drop than there are visible stars in the sky.

Iconoclastic Ice Water

I Spy Science

Your drink is cool, but if you want it to be ice cold, you'd better pop in a few blocks of frozen water. Hey, why do those ice cubes float?

Simple Science

Ice cubes float in your drink because water in its solid state is less dense than water in its liquid state. The density of a substance changes with temperature because the volume of the substance changes with temperature. Volume is a measure of how much space a substance takes up and as volume increases, density decreases. Most substances have a greater volume (lower density) when they are warmer and a lesser volume (higher density) when they are colder. In other words, the same amount of a substance will take up more space when it's warm than it does when it's cold. Water is an exception to this rule. Water has greater volume and less density when it is frozen than when it is liquid. Because the same volume of water weighs less when it is frozen, ice cubes float in your glass, and icebergs float in the ocean.

Science at Work

To demonstrate the relative densities of water in its different states, you will need a glass, red food coloring, water, an ice cube tray and vegetable oil.

Fill the ice cube tray with water. Put three drops of food coloring in one cube. Place the tray in the freezer. Fill the glass halfway with oil. When the water in the tray is frozen, pop out the colored ice cube. Drop the colored ice cube into the glass and watch what happens.

More Simple Science

The ice cube floats because it is less dense (has more mass per unit of volume) than the oil. As the ice melts, the water changes from its solid to its liquid state. Because water has less volume and greater density in its liquid state, drops of colored water form in almost perfect spheres and sink slowly through the oil (which is also less dense than liquid water) to the bottom of the glass.

Science Stunner

- Ice cubes crack when you put them in water because they are trying to shrink (change from the bigger, lighter solid state to the smaller, heavier liquid state). The shrinking exerts so much pressure on the inside of the cube that it cracks.

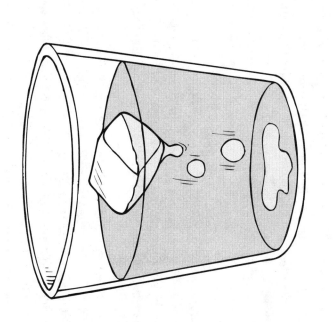

Icebergs in a Glass

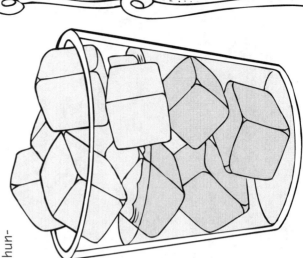

I Spy Science

You have put too many ice cubes in your glass. They're sticking up over the top. You'd better drink up, 'cause if that ice has a chance to melt, your glass will overflow. Or will it?

Science at Work

To learn about displacement, you will need: a glass, ice cubes and hot tap water.

Fill the glass with ice cubes so that the cubes stick up over the top of your glass. Pour hot tap water into the glass until it touches the rim. What happens when the ice cubes melt?

Simple Science

The glass did not overflow when the cubes melted because of the peculiar qualities of water and something called Archimedes' principle. Archimedes' principle states that an object will float when the upthrust (the force of the water pushing back against the object) acting on the object is equal to the weight of the fluid that the object displaces or pushes aside. In other words, an ice cube sinks into the water until the force of the upthrust from the water equals the weight of the cube. At this point, the weight of the ice cube and the weight of the water it displaces are equal, so it floats. Generally, things that have a large volume (the space occupied by matter) to density (a measure of the amount of matter packed into an object compared to its size) ratio are good floaters. Your ice cubes fit this description. Each ice cube has more volume and less density than the same amount of water in its liquid state. Even though each cube takes up more space than it did when it was a liquid, it is less dense–so it

weighs the same. The mass of the frozen water–the amount of matter in it–is equal to the mass of the liquid water. When the water returned to its liquid state, it took up the same amount of space in the glass–no more, no less–than the cubes displaced when they were frozen.

Science Stunners

- Archimedes (287-212 B.C.), a Greek scientist and inventor, discovered his principle one day when he overflowed the bathtub by getting into it. He was so excited by his find that he ran through the streets naked yelling, "Eureka!" ("I've got it!")
- To be classified as an iceberg–and there are more than 200,000 of them afloat in the Antarctic Ocean–a chunk of ice must stick up at least 17 feet (5 m) above the surface of the water. Anything smaller is referred to as a growler.
- Icebergs look enormous above the water (some of them are hundreds of miles long), but they are colossal below the surface. Although 90% of the volume of the ocean's icebergs is underwater, the sea level would not rise if they all suddenly melted.

Sentimental Science

- Write about a problem that was really just the "tip of the iceberg."

Activity 78

Ice: A Powerful State

I Spy Science

Listen to those cubes crack in your glass. See how they split apart in the water? What gives ice its incredible power?

Science at Work

To witness the destructive power of frozen water, you will need: an egg, a small container and a freezer.

Put the egg in the container and put the container in the freezer. Leave it overnight. Remove the container in the morning. What has happened to the egg?

Simple Science

When the watery liquid inside the egg froze, it expanded, growing enough to split the eggshell. The same thing happens when water gets into the cracks of rocks or road surfaces and then freezes. As the water changes from its liquid to its solid state and expands, it exerts enough force to crack rocks and heave pavement.

Most things on Earth contract—or shrink—when they freeze, but water does the opposite. It expands. When water molecules join together to form ice, they create a hexagonal (six-sided) shape that has an empty space in the middle. The arrangement of molecules in this ordered array, called a crystal (or lattice), takes up much more space than the loose organization of water molecules in the liquid state, which explains why ice is less dense than water (and why snowflakes are shaped the way they are).

Sentimental Science

• When you meet someone new, what do you do to "break the ice"? Make a list of great "icebreakers."

Science Stunners

• Do you know why water pipes burst in the winter? Because the water in the pipes expands as it freezes into a solid— and cracks the surrounding plastic or metal.

Hitting the Hot Spot

I Spy Science

Prefer a hot drink instead? Okay. But how are you going to deal with those first few sips, and why are they almost too hot to handle?

Science at Work

To find out why the first sip of a hot drink feels the hottest, you will need a wooden spoon, a rubber band, a plastic pill container (or film canister), a large jar, cold water, hot water, food coloring and a toothpick.

Secure the pill container to the top of the handle of the wooden spoon with the rubber band. Fill the large jar three-fourths full of cold tap water. Fill the pill container with hot tap water. Put five drops of dark food coloring in the pill container and mix with the toothpick. Lower the pill container straight down to the bottom of the larger jar. What happens to the hot colored water?

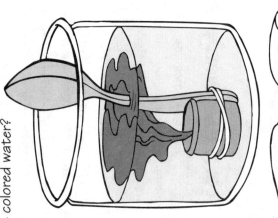

Simple Science

As the pill container made its way down into the large jar, it sent a geyser of hot water to the surface of the cold water. Even after the pill container had settled on the bottom of the jar, the hot colored water continued to rise up to the surface of the cold water and float there. The water at the bottom of the jar remained clear and colorless for a long time. Why? Water expands when it is heated. Because the hot water is less dense (has greater volume) than the cold water, it rises to the surface and hangs suspended there. Eventually, the temperature in the jar equalized, and the color mixed evenly throughout.

Science Stunner

- If you are really hot, it makes good science sense to have a hot—not cold—drink. Why? Because the hot drink will trigger your body's cooling response.

Carbonation Station

I Spy Science

Do you ever drink soda when you're thirsty? If you do, you have probably noticed that the soda foams in your glass when you add ice. So what gives carbonated drinks their fizz?

Science at Work

Soft drinks also fizz when you shake them, and there are other ways to grow a foamy head on your soda. To check out one of them, you will need an old film canister (or pill container); fresh, carbonated soda and salt.

Fill the canister half full of soda. Take the canister to the sink or to a clearing outside. Add one heaping teaspoon of salt. What happens to the soda?

Simple Science

In your experiment, the soda foams up and over the edge of the canister because of a chemical reaction that takes place between the salt and the carbon dioxide gas that is dissolved in the soda. When you added salt to the soda, it pushed some of the carbon dioxide gas out of the way. The displaced gas rose up through the soda as bubbles and made the top of the soda foamy. This bubbling-up process is called effervescence. (If you want to make your soda flat without compromising its flavor, just add a teaspoon of sugar and stir. The carbon dioxide gas goes up, up and away and the soda stays sweet.)

Science Stuff

You can trap the carbon dioxide gas as it escapes from a bottle of fresh soda with a balloon. Remove the lid from the bottle and put the balloon over the opening. Holding the balloon in place, point the bottle away from you and shake it up and down. The balloon inflates because shaking the bottle forces the carbon dioxide gas out of the soda.

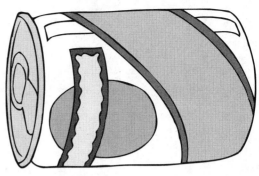

Science Stunners

- British chemist Joseph Priestly discovered oxygen and soft drinks! In 1767 Priestly figured out how to produce carbon dioxide and found that it tasted tangy and fizzed when mixed with water. But carbonated drinks didn't become popular until 1830.
- Keeping the carbon dioxide bubbles from escaping from the first carbonated drinks was a challenge. In 1892, William Painter, a machine shop operator in Baltimore, developed the "Crown Cork Bottle Seal," which prevented the beverages from going "flat." By 1920, more than 5000 soda bottlers were operating in the United States.
- Carbonated drinks were originally called seltzers, after a famous German mineral spring. Popularly known as "soft drinks"—to distinguish them from "hard" or alcoholic beverages—they were recommended as a substitute for liquor. They were nicknamed "sodas" because of the sodium bicarbonate—baking soda—used in the carbonation process. We call soda "pop" because the first drink bottles were sealed with corks that popped when they were opened.

Fun with Fizz

I Spy Science

Sodium bicarbonate—baking soda—is used to do a lot more than just carbonate your soft drinks. When mixed with other everyday substances, this useful kitchen compound almost always produces explosive results!

Science at Work

To have more fun with fizz, you will need a large, wide-mouthed jar, warm water, vinegar and dry spaghetti noodles.

Partially fill the jar with water, leaving enough room for at least two cups (500 ml) of additional liquid. Stir two tablespoons (30 ml) of baking soda into the water until dissolved. Break about five spaghetti noodles into 1/2" (1.25 cm) pieces and drop them into the jar. Slowly add 1/2 cup (120 ml) of vinegar to the jar. What happens to the spaghetti?

Simple Science

Vinegar is an acid and baking soda is a base. When you combined the two, you caused a chemical reaction (a process whereby two or more substances are changed into another substance) that produced carbon dioxide gas. Bubbles of carbon dioxide gas tend to gather on hard surfaces—think of a straw sitting in a carbonated drink. They collected in large numbers on the pieces of spaghetti. Because carbon dioxide gas is less dense than water (and because the spaghetti bits aren't very heavy), the assembled bubbles of gas rose to the surface and carried the spaghetti with them. When the bubbles surfaced, they popped, and left the spaghetti to sink back down to the bottom of the jar, where the process started all over again. (You can achieve this same effect by dropping salted peanuts into a carbonated soft drink.)

Science Stuff

You can make your own baking-soda-and-vinegar fire extinguisher. Just get a large, wide-mouth glass jar and ask an adult to punch a hole in the lid with a nail. Pour 2 cups (480 ml) of water into the jar and stir in 3 Tbsp. (45 ml) of baking soda. Put 1/2 (120 ml) cup of vinegar in a small plastic container. Float the container on the surface of the water in the jar. (Make sure the container does not spill its vinegar contents into the water.) Screw the lid on your jar. Hold the jar over the bathtub and tip it upside down. What happens? When the vinegar (acetic acid) mixes with the baking soda (sodium bicarbonate) it produces carbon dioxide gas, which foams up and spurts out of the hole in the lid of your jar. You could use that foamy spray to put out a fire!

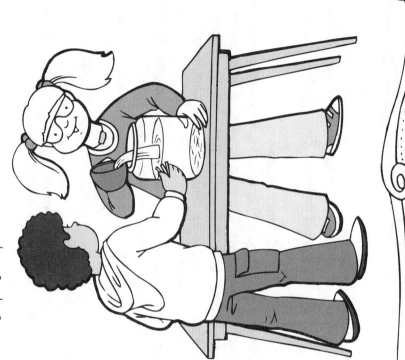

You Are What You Drink

I Spy Science

It's a good thing you finally had that drink, whatever it was—hot, cold, flavor crystal or carbonated. That's because your body was a little dehydrated after all that exercise in gym class and it needed fluid. Would anyone—or anything—else at your house care for a beverage?

Science at Work

To find out if any of the vegetables in your fridge crisper drawer are thirsty, you will need two leafy stalks of celery, two glasses of water and red and blue food coloring.

Stir 5-10 drops of red food coloring into one glass and 5-10 drops of blue food coloring into the other. Cut the bottom inch off each celery stalk and place one in each glass. Store the glasses in a safe, dark spot. Examine the leaves of the two stalks in a couple of days. What do you see? Remove the stalks from the water and again cut the bottom inch off each. Look carefully at the cut end. Do you see anything interesting?

Simple Science

The leaves of your celery had a reddish or bluish tint and when you looked at the freshly cut end, you saw rows of tiny circles outlined in red or blue. These circles are the cut ends of the long, thin tubes of linked xylem cells that travel all the way up the celery stalk. The colored water moved up these tubes to the leaves of the celery through a process called capillary action, which allows water molecules to creep between the spaces of other materials. And because water tends to climb a little ways up the walls of certain substances—like a dry paper towel or the side of a glass—new water molecules move up into the celery stalk to replace those that evaporate from the leaves. Water molecules cling together, and when they're squeezed into narrow tubes they grip even more tightly—with enough strength to pull other water molecules up behind them. Because this action is possible only if the tubes are full of liquid to begin with, trees and other plants start out life as seedlings with liquid-filled tubes! But why did you have to keep your celery in the dark? To speed up the results! Plants make food in their leaves during the day while the sun is shining. They drink at night when the sun goes down.

Science Stuff

• Do cut flowers need water? To find out, buy a white carnation. Cut the bottom 1/2" (1.25 cm) off the stem; then cut the stem lengthways from the fresh cut halfway up to the flower. Place two glasses side by side—one with red water, one with blue—and put half of the stem in each glass. What do you see in a few days' time?

Science Stunners

• Plants need water. Through transpiration, water travels up through a plant's roots and stems and evaporates into the air from its leaves and flowers. Through translocation, water carries food away from the leaves and into the buds, shoots and roots.

• Some trees "drink" more than 2000 pounds (1000 kg) of water every day!

Let the Sunshine In

I Spy Science

So plants drink water—and need water to live and grow—but do they really need light? After all, your celery stalks did okay in the dark.

Science at Work

To find out how important light is to healthy plant development, you will need six dried beans, a glass of water, a paper towel, two small containers, small stones, potting soil and water.

Scrunch the paper towel and push the beans into it. Place the paper towel in the glass and cover with water. Soak the beans in this fashion overnight. The next day, put about 1" (2.5 cm) of stones in each container. Fill the rest of the container with potting soil. Poke three 1" (2.5 cm) holes in the soil of each container. Put one bean in each hole and cover with soil. Water the soil until it is moist but not wet. Put one container in a sunny spot and the other in a dark cupboard. Look at the containers every day and sprinkle with water if the soil becomes dry. Is there a difference between the bean plants growing in the two containers?

Simple Science

After a few days of growth, the bean plants in the sun probably looked green and healthy. The plants in the closet, however, were very pale and probably taller than their counterparts. Plants need light to make food. To make sure that they get the light they need, plant cells are equipped with special light receptors. When these receptors don't get enough light, they signal the plant to grow long and thin in an effort to seek some. The plants in the closet were pale because there wasn't enough light available for them to produce chlorophyll (which gives them their green color and enables them to absorb sunlight and produce food). Once moved to a nice sunny location, these sickly plants will soon turn green and start to grow more proportionately.

Sentimental Science

- Could you live without light? How would it feel to be trapped in a dark place for days on end?

Science Stunner

- Photosynthesis is a process that occurs in all green plants, generally in the leaves. Many of the cells in a leaf contain tiny organelles called chloroplasts. The chlorophyll and other pigments in the chloroplasts collect energy from sunlight and through a series of complicated chemical reactions use this trapped energy to turn water and carbon dioxide into a simple sugar called glucose. The glucose is used to fuel the plant's cells and to make other substances, such as starch and cellulose.

Grow Towards the Light, My Spud

I Spy Science

Okay. Plants need light–even seek out light. But to what lengths will a plant g(r)o(w) to find a spot in the sun?

Science at Work

To find out just how determined plants are to find a light source, you will need a shoe box, cardboard, scissors, tape, water, a small container, potting soil, a potato (or bean) sprout and small stones.

Center and cut a 1" (2.5 cm) hole in one end of the shoe box, about 1" (2.5 cm) in from the edge. Cut four cardboard strips that are the same height as the shoe box but 1" (2.5 cm) narrower. Tape the cardboard strips to the inside of the box to create an alternating maze pattern. Put the small stones in the bottom of the container and cover with potting soil. Cut the end off a sprouting potato and push it down into the soil so that the sprout sticks up. Cover the potato with soil (leave a bit of the sprout poking out) and stand the container in the shoe box at the opposite end of the hole. (You can lay down the box or stand it on end for this experiment.) Water the potato and put the lid on the box. Put the box in a nice, sunny spot. When the sprout pokes out of the hole–no peeking inside the box!–remove the lid. (Make sure that someone (not you) gives your potato a little water every day while it is growing.)

Simple Science

Very little light found its way into the shoe box, the potato plant weaved its way through the maze to reach it. The emerged sprout was still white (as it was when you retrieved it from the bag in your cupboard) because there was not enough light for the plant to produce chlorophyll.

Sentimental Science

- Imagine that you are the potato sprout. Describe your journey toward the light and your eventual triumph.

Science Stunner

- Plants can't talk, but they can communicate. A plant that is damaged by an insect, for example, can release a hormone in the form of a gas. Nearby plants that take in this hormone receive advanced warning of an attack and can better defend themselves against.

Upside Up; Downside Down

I Spy Science

No matter how high you hold your head, your feet remain firmly rooted to the ground. You always return to an upright position. This is true for plants, too. While light directs the growth of a plant's stem, gravity keeps its roots in check.

Science at Work

To see how gravity affects root growth, you will need four bean seeds, a large glass, blotting paper and water.

Put the beans in the glass and soak in water overnight. In the morning, empty the glass and line it with the blotting paper. Fill the glass with water and let it sit for about 20 seconds. Dump the water out. The blotting paper should be thoroughly wet. Place the seeds between the glass and the blotting paper spaced evenly around the cup about one inch (2.5 cm) from the top. Make sure to put the four beans in different positions: two horizontal (one "belly button" facing up, the other facing down) and two vertical (one "belly button" facing left, the other facing right). Keep a little water in the bottom of the cup at all times so that capillary action keeps the blotting paper wet, and don't put the cup in direct sunlight. How do the seeds grow? After your bean plants have grown above the top of the cup, lay the cup on its side and let the beans continue to grow. (You'll have to stand your cup up for a few minutes each day to wet the blotting paper.) What happens to the roots and stems?

Simple Science

You don't have to worry about planting seeds right side up. No matter how a seed is positioned, its roots grow down and its stem grows up. That's because there are special growth hormones in plants that respond to the Earth's gravitational pull. This response is called *geotropism*, which is Greek for "turning to Earth."

Sentimental Science

• Think about the definition of a root: "the underground portion of a plant which absorbs moisture, obtains or stores nourishment and provides support," or more generally, "that from which anything derives origin, growth or life and vigor." Write about your "roots."

Science Stunner

• Have you ever noticed that plants always bend towards the light? This bending is a hormonal response. Hormones gather on the side of the stem that is turned away from the light, making it bend.

Vacuum Packed

I Spy Science

All of this plant science might help you out at home—if taking care of houseplants is one of your pleasures or chores. And speaking of chores . . . you'd better get out the vacuum cleaner, because you spilled some soil on the floor when you were potting your veggies!

Simple Science

Do you recall the "empty isn't really empty" rule from Activity 29? Well, like most rules there is an exception to it. And that exception is a vacuum. When you stick a suction cup to the wall, you create a vacuum by squeezing all the air molecules out from between the cup and the wall. There is no air and therefore no air pressure under the suction cup, so when the air pressure in the room pushes against the outside of the suction cup, there is nothing underneath to push back. The vacuum under the suction cup makes it possible for the air molecules in the room to press the cup securely to the wall. (Eventually air will push in through tiny gaps between the wall and the suction cup, eliminating the vacuum, and the cup will fall off the wall.) When you suck liquid through a drinking straw, you create a vacuum by removing the air molecules from the straw. As long as you maintain the vacuum, the air pressure from the room will press down on the surface of the liquid and force it up the straw and into your mouth. Your vacuum cleaner works in much the same way. A motor inside the vacuum cleaner blows almost all of the air out of the machine, creating a partial vacuum inside the machine. The air in the

room then rushes in to fill the empty space by entering the vacuum cleaner hose. The rushing air carries dirt up off the floor and into the machine.

Science at Work

To create your own vacuum in a glass, you will need a piece of cardboard, a glass and water.

Fill the glass with water. Moisten a piece of cardboard and place it over the mouth of the glass. Hold the cardboard firmly against the glass and tip the works upside down. Take your hand off the cardboard. (You'd better do this over a sink, just in case.) Does the cardboard fall off the glass?

More Simple Science

The little space that appeared between the bottom of the glass and the top of the water is a vacuum. Because there is no air in the space, there is no air pressure to push down on the water. But there is lots of air outside the glass—and therefore lots of air pressure. The outside air pushes up against the cardboard, "sticking" it to the glass and preventing the water from pouring out.

Suggestive Science

- Has your mind ever been a vacuum? Do you sometimes feel like you live in a vacuum? Use science to suggest a meaning for these expressions.

Activity 87

Taking a Shine

I Spy Science

Is polishing the furniture on your chore list? Too bad. It would take a lot less elbow grease to shine those dirty old pennies in your pocket.

Science at Work

To polish up your copper, you will need an old, dirty penny; a soft rag; vinegar and salt.

Pour some vinegar on the rag. Sprinkle a little salt into the vinegar. Place the penny in the salt and rub it between your thumb and index finger with the cloth for about 20 seconds. Rinse the penny with some clean tap water. How does the penny look?

Simple Science

The dirty old penny shined up like new! The salt (sodium chloride) and the vinegar (acetic acid) chemically reacted to form a weak solution of hydrochloric acid. In this solution, the sodium and chlorine molecules lose their tight grip on each other. The chlorine is attracted to the copper and pushes the dirt chemicals out of its way to get to the penny underneath. When you rinsed the penny in the tap water, you stopped the chemical reaction. Over time, the penny will dull and darken (oxidize) again due to its contact with the water and oxygen molecules in the air.

Science Stuff

Here's a neat way to polish your tarnished silver coins. Dissolve one teaspoon each of salt and baking soda in a small amount of water and submerse the coins in the solution. With the help of an adult, put some water on the stove in a glass or enamel pot. Tear a small strip of aluminum foil into pieces and add the pieces to the water. Bring the water to a boil and remove the pot from the heat. When the water has cooled, pop in your coins for an electrolyte rinse. Dry the coins with a paper towel. Your silver change is shiny and clean because of several chemical reactions. The salt and soda loosened the tarnish and heat turned the water and aluminum foil into an electrolyte solution, which carried a mild electric charge that lifted the tarnish.

Sentimental Science

- Write about a time when your talents shone.
- List five things in your life that could use a little polishing.

Suggestive Science

- Has anyone ever told you that you "shine up like a new penny"? (Is this an insult or a compliment? Explain.) What happens when someone "takes a shine to you"?

Activity 88

Don't Cry over Chopped Onions

I Spy Science

You've vacuumed up the potting soil, polished the furniture—and your pennies—and you're ready for a little rest and relaxation before dinner. Unfortunately, your services are required immediately in the kitchen. There seems to be a problem. The chef is in tears. But why? Chopping an onion isn't all that sad!

Simple Science

When you cut an onion, the unusual sulphur compounds it contains react with oxygen in the air and form powerfully odoriferous chemicals. To keep the strong, burning chemicals away from your eyes, your body produces tears. It takes about 30 seconds from the time the onion is first cut until the chemical reactions occur, and the whole tearful episode is over in about five minutes. Unless you cut another onion!

Science at Work

There are a few things you can do to inhibit the spread of the stinky molecules and keep them away from your eyes. Because the chemicals are water soluble (dissolve in water), if you cut the onion while holding it under water, most of the chemicals will go down the drain and not into the air. Heating or freezing the onion prior to chopping slows down the reaction between the sulphur compounds and the enzymes. And you can also dice your onions in a breezy spot, or use a fan to disperse the chemicals. The next time your dinner calls for chopped onions, try one of these interventions. Does it work?

Science Stuff

- There are lots of old wives' tales that offer advice on chopping onions without tears. One is to chew on a stale crust of bread while you slice and dice. Have you heard of any others? Test one. Is there some truth to the tale?

Suggestive Science

- Do other foods, like milk, make you cry? If not, why do people "cry over spilt milk"? What does this expression mean? Have you ever cried over spilt milk?

Science Stunners

- Different kinds of onions contain different amounts and types of sulphur. The odor of some onions is harsher than others, so you can choose your onion according to your tolerance of its smell!

- All the tears are worth it. Onions taste great, are loaded with nutrients (including vitamins B, C and G) and have anti-inflammatory, antiallergic and anti-asthmatic properties.

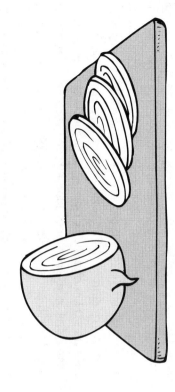

Cut and Paste Platelets

I Spy Science

Hopefully whoever was cutting the onions for dinner didn't cut a finger as well. If he or she did, the wound is probably starting to heal already. How?

Simple Science

Trillions of fragile platelets move continuously through your blood vessels. When you cut your skin, it releases substances into the blood that make the nearby platelets sticky. These platelets join together and adhere to the edges of the cut to create a plug. At the same time, a protein in the blood called fibrinogen changes into fibrin. The fibrin weaves a dense criss-crossing network of long, sticky threads over the cut, which contract and bind the red blood cells together to form a clot. The clot prevents red blood cells from leaking out and new germs from getting in, but allows white blood cells to sneak through to attack any invaders that are already established. When the clot dries out, it forms a scab. The scab acts like a bandage and lets new skin grow underneath. When the skin has healed, the scab falls off. Thank goodness for platelets. If your blood didn't clot, it would flow for a long time.

Science at Work

To make and heal an artificial wound, you will need measuring spoons, two cups, cornstarch, a spoon, soy sauce, water, white corn syrup, red food coloring, petroleum jelly, toilet paper and cocoa powder.

Measure ½ tsp. (2.5 ml) of cornstarch into the cup. Stir in about 10 drops of soy sauce, and slowly add 1 tsp. (5 ml) of water. Stir in 2 tsp. (10 ml) corn syrup and two drops of food coloring. Put a drop of the mixture on your forearm. Does it remind you of anything? Clean your arm with a paper towel and mix ¼ tsp. (1.25 ml) of your fake blood with ½ tsp. (2.5 ml) of petroleum jelly. Put a blob of the mixture on your arm. Press on strips of toilet paper until the wound is covered. Spread a thin layer of your blood goop over the toilet paper. Sprinkle with cocoa. What have you got?

Sentimental Science

• Describe the worst cut you ever had. How did it happen? How did it heal? Did the wound leave a scar?

Science Stunners

• Blood is incredible. The 6½ pints (4 liters) that you have in your body carry oxygen to the cells in your body; transport food, hormones, waste products and heat and defend your body against disease.

• One drop of blood contains millions of cells. Most of these are red blood cells, which get their color from a pigment called hemoglobin. Some crustaceans have blue blood. Instead of hemoglobin, their bodies contain the respiratory pigment hemocyanin (which contains copper).

• Your body is constantly fighting off germs. White blood cells (outnumbered by red cells 45:1) rush around killing and eating germs. Some engulf foreign cells (like bacteria) whole; others release antibodies that attack intruders (such as viruses).

Activity 90

Kitchen Conductors

I Spy Science

The onions are chopped, any resulting injuries are clotting and you're ready to cook. But that lid seems to be glued to the sauce jar! How on Earth are you going to get it off?

Simple Science

If the lid is stuck, just run it under hot tap water for half a minute or so and try again. It should twist off easily. That's because metal is a better conductor of heat than glass, so the lid expands more quickly under the hot water than the jar.

Science at Work

To test the conductivity of a few of the materials found in your kitchen, you will need a plastic spoon, a wooden spoon, a stainless steel spoon, (a silver spoon) butter or lard, raisins, a large heat-proof jar or glass and boiling water.

Make sure your spoons are roughly the same thickness and height. Stick a raisin to the top of the handle of each spoon using a bit of butter. Put the spoons, raisin-sides up, in the glass. (Make sure the raisins are all at the same height when the spoons are in the glass.) Ask a grown-up to pour in a few inches of boiling water. (Don't let the water touch the spoon handles.) What happens to the raisins?

More Simple Science

Some of the spoons transferred or conducted heat better than others. The good conductors moved the heat energy in the water up the spoon handles more quickly than the poor conductors, and thus melted the butter (which released the raisin) faster. To check the conductivity of glass, carefully touch a finger to the rim of the glass and then to the tip of each spoon handle. How does the glass compare to each of the other materials? Do your observations support the lid-and-jar theory?

Suggestive Science

Have you heard these expressions, "If you can't stand the heat, get out of the kitchen," and "Out of the frying pan and into the fire"? What do they mean? Could you use these expressions appropriately to describe a time in your life?

Science Stunner

• Have you ever wondered why onions sizzle and spit in the pan? It's because they contain water. When you put the pieces of onion in the hot pan, they release tiny drops of water. When these drops hit the hot pan, the water molecules inside of them speed up, causing the drops to dance around before evaporating into little puffs of water vapor. The dancing and exploding make waves of sound that travel through the air to your ears and are heard as a sizzling sound.

Butterballs

I Spy Science

If that sauce jar is empty, don't put it in the recycling bin just yet. Wash it out and use it to whip up a little homemade butter for your dinner.

Science at Work

To make your own butter, you will need a jar (with lid), a measuring cup, whipping cream, water and a spoon.

Pour 1 cup (250 ml) of whipping cream into the jar. In about 10 minutes, screw on the lid and start to shake the jar vigorously. After a while (be patient, this takes plenty of time and lots of energy), you should start to see a change in the cream. It will become foamy and white. Soon, tiny granules of butter will start to form. When the granules are about the size of your baby fingernail, stop shaking. Pour off the liquid (called buttermilk) into the measuring cup and rinse the globules of butter under cold tap water. Put the globs in a dish and press them together with the spoon. If you like your butter salted, add a few sprinkles from your table shaker and work it evenly through the ball. You can even shape your butter before putting it in the fridge or press a fancy design into the top. (If you're feeling lazy, you can substitute an electric mixer for your muscle power. Just whip the cream on high in a chilled bowl for about 7-9 minutes until you see yellow clumps. Pour off the liquid and continue to mix until a butterball forms.)

Simple Science

Cream is a suspension, a combination of butterfat molecules (solids) and water (a liquid). The butterfat floats throughout (is suspended in) the water. When you shook the cream in the jar, you added energy and forced the butterfat molecules to collide and stick together. When enough of these molecules were forced together, they formed solid globules of fat and separated from the water. After pouring off the liquid and mashing the individual globs together, you ended up with one big, delicious ball of fat-butter. How much of the cream was liquid (buttermilk) and how much was solid (butter)?

Science Stunner

- Is the butter you made lighter or darker than store-bought butter? The color of butter depends on the kind of cow that made the buttermilk and what the cow was eating at the time. Because people expect their butter to look the same all the time, dairies usually use food coloring to dye it a standard yellow.

On Dirty Dishes and Detergents

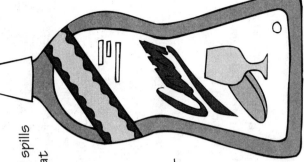

I Spy Science

You've finished your dinner, and now you're ready to tackle the dishes. But how are you going to get rid of all that food grease?

Science at Work

To watch your dishwashing soap do its stuff, you will need a glass jar, water, vegetable oil and dishwashing soap.

Put 1/4 cup (60 ml) of oil in the jar. Add 3/4 cup (180 ml) of water. What happens to the oil and water? Put the lid on the jar and shake it vigorously. Now what happens? Remove the lid and add a little squirt of dishwashing liquid. Put the lid back on and shake again. What happens this time?

Simple Science

When you put the oil and water in the jar, the oil (which is less dense than the water) floated to the top. When you shook the jar, the oil and water mixed briefly, but they separated again as soon as you stopped shaking. Oil and water do not mix. They are immiscible. Detergents like your dishwashing soap break large drops of oil into much smaller droplets and allow them to hang suspended throughout another liquid. When you added dishwashing soap to the oil and water and shook the jar, a milky colored emulsion formed. (Given your knowledge of emulsions, how does dishwashing soap help you to clean your greasy dinner dishes?)

Sentimental Science

- Does it help to break an overwhelmingly large project down into smaller, more manageable chunks that can be worked on individually? Describe how you might "chunk" a project on an ancient civilization.

- What happens when an oil tanker spills its contents into the ocean? What might be done to clean up the spill? Would it be a good idea to use an emulsifier? Why or why not?

Science Stuff

- Oil and vinegar dressing is a temporary emulsion. Like oil and water, oil and vinegar do not mix. When you put the two in a jar, the oil floats on top of the vinegar. Shake the jar and the two mix. Stop shaking and they separate.

Science Stunner

- Mayonnaise is an oil and vinegar emulsion. The emulsifier is egg yolk.

Activity 93

Breaking the Tension

I Spy Science

When you put plastic lids and containers into the dishwater, do some of them sit on the surface until you push them under? What keeps them from sinking?

Science at Work

Surface tension keeps the plastic from sinking. To see surface tension in action, you will need a glass, water and a dropper.

Fill the glass to the rim with water. Use the dropper to add water to the glass, drop by drop. What happens? What if you keep adding drops of water?

Simple Science

Water molecules have a strong attraction to one another. Inside the glass, the water molecules surround one another and they pull toward one another equally in all directions. But the molecules at the surface have no water above them; they can only be pulled by the water particles beside and below them. There is nothing to pull them upwards, only inward and downward. This tension creates an invisible elastic-like skin at the water's surface, a characteristic that is called surface tension. When you added more drops of water to the full glass, the surface tension was strong enough to keep the water from spilling over, even when the water bulged quite a bit above it. Eventually the volume of water above the rim of the glass got to be too great. It broke the surface tension and the water spilled out of the glass.

Science Stuff

- Make a loop with your index finger and thumb. Dip the loop in some clean soapy dishwater. Carefully lift the loop. Can you see a thin soap film? Blow gently into the middle of the loop. By filling the soap film with enough air to float away, you should be able to make a bubble. How does it work? When you add dishwashing soap to water, you loosen the hold that the water molecules have on one another. This makes the water "stretchy."

Suggestive Science

- Have you ever said or done anything to break (or diffuse) the tension during an awkward moment? Have you ever been in a strained or anxious situation with other people—one in which you could "cut the tension with a knife"? Use science to describe such situations. (Hint: tension is "the act of stretching, the condition of being stretched tight.")

Science Stunners

- Some insects, such as water striders, are so light that they can actually walk on water. They are not heavy enough to break the surface tension of the water.
- Why does dishwashing soap bubble so much? Because there's more soap in the water than dirt. When soap and water mix together, they make a film. This film traps the dirt and slides it off the dishes. When there is more soap than dirt, the extra soap film traps air instead and makes bubbles!
- Most bubbles are spherical because surface tension pulls them into this shape.

Down the Drain

I Spy Science

You've done the dishes and drained the water. Now comes the gross part: cleaning the drain basket. What is all that mushy stuff anyway? It doesn't look much like food.

Science at Work

To find out what happens to your food in the dishwater, you will need a dish, a raisin, a dried bean, a dried pea and a bread crust.

Fill the dish with warm water. Add the raisin, dried bean, dried pea and bread crust. Check your dish frequently over the next few hours. What happens to the food?

Simple Science

Raisins are partially dehydrated, which means they have lost most of the moisture they had when they were grapes. Dried beans and peas have lost all their moisture and are completely dehydrated. When you put the dried-out fruit and vegetables and bread crust in the water, they started to take in moisture. As their tissues expanded, they grew larger. The more water they absorbed, the bigger they got, until they swelled up to nearly their original size. (The bread crust grew to be even larger than its "dry" size.) The gross stuff in your drain basket is soggy and slimy because it has absorbed so much moisture from the dishwater.

Sentimental Science

- People get wrinkly, too, just like the food in your drain basket—but for different reasons. As your skin ages, fibers in the dermis, or thick "underskin," break down, causing lines and wrinkles to appear as the skin loses its stretchy, elastic texture. Describe the wrinkly face of someone you know and love.

- Imagine that you are small enough to be sucked down the drain. Write a descriptive paragraph detailing such a journey.

Suggestive Science

- Have you ever heard the expression "down the drain"? What does it mean?

Science Stunners

- Many people believe that global positioning determines which way water swirls down the drain. In fact, it is the shape of the bowl and the motion of the water before the drain is opened that determines the direction of the whirlpool. There is too little water in your sink or tub to be affected by the Earth's spinning.

- That funny sucking noise you hear when the last bit of water drains from your bathtub is caused by a vacuum. The drainpipe is like a drinking straw. You create a vacuum when you suck on a drinking straw. But when you get to the bottom of the glass, there isn't enough juice left to maintain the vacuum and air rushes up the straw to fill the gap. The juice and air slosh together and make that slurping noise—just like the last few drops of water and the air do as they rush down your drainpipe.

Moviemaker Magic

I Spy Science

Dinner's done and so are the dishes. It's finally time to relax. But why watch a movie on TV when you can make your own?

Science at Work

To make your own movie magic, you will need two index or recipe file cards, a marker, a straw and cellophane tape.

Use the marker to draw a simple picture on the first card (a smiley face perhaps). Making sure your two cards and the images on them line up exactly, copy the same picture onto the second card with a slight change (swap a frown for the smile; closed eyes for open eyes). Secure the straw to the back of one card using lots of tape. Position the second card over the first, faceup, and tape the two cards together. Hold the straw between the palms of your hands and twirl it by rubbing your hand back and forth against one another. Try twirling the straw at different speeds. What do you see? (Try other picture combinations. Draw a bird and a cage; a dog and a doghouse; a goldfish and a bowl. Can you put the bird behind bars, the dog in its house or the fish under glass?)

Simple Science

The scientific principles that make your home movie magic work are the same as those used to produce movies for big screen theater. When you look at one picture and then quickly flip to the other, your brain remembers the first picture for a split second and blends it with the second. Known as "persistence of vision," it is this visual ability that makes the still-frame pictures in movies "move." If a light flashes on and off more than 30 times in a single second, your brain sees it as a steady beam of light. At the movies, the screen is dark about 50% of the

time. But because the film projector is flickering 72 separate bright picture images at the screen every second, you don't notice the darkness between the frames: your brain blends the flickering picture frames together to make one continuous motion picture.

More Simple Science

You can make a movie flip book using a stapled recipe card booklet or a small pad of paper. Just make sure that you draw your figure in the same place on each card or page and change the figure only slightly from one page to the next. (To watch your movie, hold the joined edge of you booklet or pad between the thumb and forefinger of one hand and flip the pages with the thumb and forefinger of the other hand.)

Science Stunners

According to Guinness World Records 2000:

- The most expensive movie ever made was Twentieth Century Fox's 1997 blockbuster hit *Titanic*, which cost $250 million to produce. It is also one of the most profitable, having grossed $1.835 billion worldwide in just 11½ years.

- The 20 James Bond films, based on novels by Iam Flemming and featuring British secret agent 007–otherwise known as James Bond–have grossed more than $1 billion worldwide, making them the most profitable film series ever. It is estimated that more than half the people on Earth have seen at least one Bond film.

- The classic fairy tale *Cinderella* is the most filmed story in the world. The movie appears on-screen in 95 different versions.

- William Shakespeare is the most filmed author in history. Three hundred and fifty movies have been made based on his plays.

- The largest movie studio complex is Universal City in Los Angeles, California. With 561 buildings and 34 soundstages, the studio occupies 420 acres.

Your Yawn Caught On

I Spy Science

It's late and it's been a long day. You must be bushed. Is that why you're yawning?

Simple Science

We know that a yawn is a slow breath, but we don't really know what causes it. Some scientists think we yawn when we're bored or tired. Others think we yawn because there isn't enough oxygen in the air. Still others believe that we yawn to put more oxygen into our bloodstream by stretching our neck and breathing muscles. Because most of us yawn when we're falling asleep or waking up, one popular theory is that a good yawn gives us a fresh lungful of air when our breathing is shallow. Yawning seems to be contagious or catching; if you see someone else yawn you will probably yawn, too—although there are people who can talk themselves out of it. One theory describes contagious yawning as a social function. In apes, the sight or sound of one troop member yawning tends to get the rest of the troop yawning. It could serve to bind the troop together or to signal the apes to find shelter for the night. If the apes all went into the trees to find a sleeping place at the same time, it would help to secure their safety.

Science at Work

Do you think yawning is contagious? Does just hearing or reading the word yawn make it happen? Are you yawning now? What if the person on the other end of the phone line yawns? Do you? Try yawning when you are around other people. Do they start yawning too? Can anyone resist the urge? Keep track of your results and see if you can come to any solid conclusions.

Sentimental Science

- Have you ever been unable to stop yawning? Has this problem ever caused you any embarrassment?

Suggestive Science

- Have you ever heard of a "yawning cavity"? Have you ever seen one? Would this expression be a fitting description for your mouth? Why or why not?

Bacteria Brush-Off

I Spy Science

You're tired, but don't even think about going to bed without brushing your teeth. Not unless you want them to soak in an acid mouthwash all night, that is.

Science at Work

To see how easily acid can eat through your teeth, which are made primarily of calcium, you will need a jar, vinegar and an uncooked egg.

Fill the jar with vinegar. Put the egg in the jar and soak for 24 hours. Remove the egg. How does it feel?

Simple Science

When you took the egg out of the vinegar, the shell had completely dissolved and the egg felt soft and rubbery. (Drop it from a short height into your sink. It bounces like a ball.) An eggshell is almost entirely calcium carbonate, and vinegar is acetic acid. When you put the egg in the vinegar, the acetic acid reacted with the calcium carbonate in the shell and caused it to "decalcify," or dissolve, much like the acid in your mouth dissolves the calcium in your teeth. You have to brush your teeth to get rid of the little bits of food that stick to them after you eat. If you don't, the bacteria living in your mouth feed on the sugar in the leftovers and produce acid as a waste product. The acid is strong enough to melt (or decay) the tough outer covering of your teeth and the slightly softer dentine layer below, creating holes called cavities. By brushing your teeth, you get rid of the sugars that the bacteria like to eat. And if the bacteria have nothing to eat, they don't produce waste. No waste, no acid, no cavities!

Science Stuff

- If you want to find the spots that your toothbrush didn't reach, just swish a little food coloring around in your mouth after brushing. (Make sure to spit the food coloring out; don't swallow it.) The color sticks best to plaque—the bacteria on your teeth—so look for the darkest spots.

Science Stunners

- The surface of your teeth, which is made of enamel, is the hardest part of your body.
- The teeth at the front of your mouth—the incisors and cuspids—are used for biting and tearing. Your bicuspids and molars (at the sides and back of your mouth) are used for chewing, grinding and crushing. Is it possible to tear with your back teeth and grind with your front?
- The leading cause of death among wild elephants is worn-out teeth.
- Thousands of years later, we can tell what primitive children ate because of the shape of their teeth and the tiny marks and scratches on their surfaces. They did not eat refined sugar, so they had virtually no tooth decay. Their food was rough, however, so their teeth were well worn.

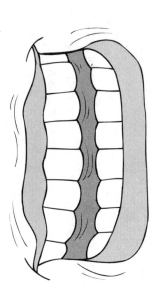

Friction Footsies

I Spy Science

Your clean teeth feel great—and so does climbing into bed. But your feet are freezing! No problem. Just give them a vigorous rub together or slide them back and forth on the bottom sheet and they'll be warmed up in no time. It's a friction fact.

Science at Work

To see friction in action, you will need a long pencil.

Rest the pencil at the base of your left index finger so that just less than 1/2 of the eraser end of the pencil sticks out to the left beyond your finger. Position the base of your right index finger directly below the right end of the pencil. With your thumbs sticking up at a 90° angle, try to bring your two hands toward each other in a praying position. Do both hands move under the pencil? What happens to the pencil?

Simple Science

When you try to bring your two hands together under the pencil, friction keeps your left hand in place and prevents the pencil from falling. Friction is a force that occurs whenever one surface rubs against another. Because surfaces that are in close contact grip, all objects resist moving across one another, and this resistance is called friction. As the amount of contact between two objects increases, so does friction. And the heavier the weight of the object on top, the greater the friction between it and the object upon which it is resting. The pencil was heavier at the long end, so there was more friction between it and your left index finger. While friction prevented your left hand from moving, your right hand slid to

meet it. Your two hands met in the middle and the pencil stayed balanced.

Friction always opposes motion. When you rubbed your feet together or on the sheet, you expended energy. This "lost" energy "reappeared" as heat and sound. The heat warmed up your feet.

Science Stunners

- When the tires of your bike are underinflated, more of the tire comes in contact with the road. This extra contact increases the friction between the road surface and your tires and makes it harder for you to pedal your bike.
- Car tire manufacturers are very conscious of the important effects of friction on driving safety. The greater the amount of rubber in contact with the pavement, the more the tire will "stick" to the road, which offers a definite traction control advantage (especially when cornering at high speed). But what happens when it rains? If a film of water gets sandwiched between the tire and the road, friction is lost and so are traction and steering. Hence the raised tire tread. Tire treads are designed to channel water away from the tire, which allows it to stay in contact with the road surface in wet weather and maintain friction.

Lunar Lingo

I Spy Science

Can you see the moon out your bedroom window? What shape is it tonight?

Science at Work

To simulate the phases of the moon in your bedroom, you will need aluminum foil, a craft stick and a lamp (without a shade).

Make a loose ball out of aluminum foil. This will be your moon. Stick a craft stick into the middle of the moon. Turn on the lamp and put it on a table in the middle of the room so that the bulb is at eye level. (You might have to kneel down.) Face the lamp, holding the moon by the craft stick at arm's length just above your head between the sun (the lamp) and the Earth (you). How does the side of the ball that is facing you appear? Slowly turn counterclockwise on the spot. What happens to the ball as you turn?

Simple Science

As you turned, the surface of the ball was exposed to different levels of light from the bulb. The "Earth" made one complete revolution around the "sun," and the "moon" passed through all of its phases. At first, the side of the ball that was facing you was dark. This was the first phase of the moon—the "new moon"—and the moon was not visible. As the moon orbited the Earth, more and more of its surface received light from the sun and was revealed. The second phase (when you had made one-quarter of a revolution) was the "first quarter moon" or "crescent moon," when a sliver of moon could be seen on the right. The third phase (after you had made half a revolution and stood directly between the

sun and the moon) was the "full moon"—when the whole of the moon was visible. The fourth phase (after three-fourths of a revolution) was the "last quarter moon" or "crescent moon," when a sliver of moon could be seen on the left.

Sentimental Science

• Write part of a full moon werewolf story—the part where your best friend turns into a frightening, furry creature right before your very eyes!

Science Stunners

• Earth, like many planets, has a satellite: the moon. The moon orbits Earth once every 29½ days. With no air and no water on its surface, the moon is boiling hot during the day and freezing cold at night.

• On July 20, 1969, the American spacecraft Apollo 11 landed on the moon, 384,000 miles away from Earth. A few hours later, astronaut Neil Armstrong became the first human being to walk on its surface. Since that auspicious day in history, 11 other Americans have walked, worked and slept on the moon.

Because there is no wind or rain on the moon, the footprints of these astronauts will remain on the surface of our satellite for a long, long time.

Activity 100

Constellation Creations

I Spy Science

As you gaze at the night sky, can you see the patterns of human and creature shapes among the stars? If you can, you are not alone.

Simple Science

Even though their position in the sky constantly changes with the Earth's rotation, the stars in our galaxy and the patterns they make remain fixed in relation to one another. People have used the stars to navigate for centuries, and ancient astronomers saw and named patterns in the stars–generally mythological characters and creatures complete with their own complex folklore–called constellations. Since 1925, the International Astronomical Union has officially recognized 88 constellations, or groupings, of stars in the night sky, the easiest of which to identify are the Big and Little Dippers.

(Sentimental) Science at Work

To make your own constellation, you will need graph paper, a pen and a pencil.

Mark every point where two lines intersect on the graph paper with a pen mark. These are the stars in your night sky. Connect the dots–or stars–to create your own constellation or asterism (any pattern of stars that is distinctive enough to be easily remembered). Name your constellation and write a myth to explain its significance.

Science Stunners

- You can see about 3000 stars with your naked eye, but there are millions more that you can't see even with the most powerful telescope.
- Our galaxy, the Milky Way, contains about 100,000 million stars, and ours is just one of millions of galaxies in the universe.
- The next closest star to our own–the sun–is Proxima Centauri, which is about 25 trillion miles away.
- Although the stars in a constellation seem to be fixed at the same distance from Earth, they can, in fact, be millions of light years distance from one another.

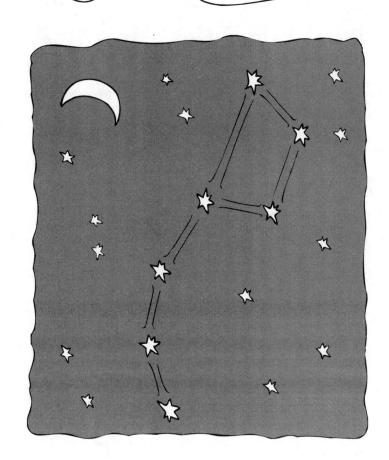

Dream Weavers

I Spy Science

The day is over, but you still have important work to do . . . in your sleep!

Simple Science

When you fall asleep, your conscious brain shuts down, but—your heart and lungs, for example, your subconscious brain keeps working—controlling to keep you alive all through the night. Even in your state of near-unconsciousness, you are doing important work: your body is being restored; your tissues are repairing themselves; your cells are being renewed and you are growing. When you first shut your eyes at night, you slip into a deep sleep. In this state, body processes such as heartbeat and breathing slow down, and your muscles relax. After a while, however, everything speeds up slightly. Your muscles twitch and your eyes move under closed lids. This is REM, or rapid eye movement, sleep: the time when dreams usually occur. (The REM state accounts for 18% of the sleep of children ages 21 months to 19 years, 13% of the sleep of people ages 20 to 29 years and only 3% of the sleep of people ages 50 to 69 years.) Then you go into a deep sleep again, and so on, throughout the night. Each night you pass through four or five cycles of nondream and dream sleep, with each complete cycle accounting for 80 to 100 minutes of your full night's slumber.

Science at Work

For the next week, keep a dream diary beside your bed. As soon as you wake up—in the night or in the morning—write down in your diary as much as you can remember about your dreams. At the end of the week, write a short story based on your most interesting dream. (Do you tend to remember your dreams or forget them? Do you have lots of "short" dreams or one or two "long" ones? Are your dreams gritty, realistic and sensible or soft, surreal and weird?)

Science Stunners

- Your body follows a day/night or "circadian" rhythm. Your body clock is set at about 25 hours, which is very close to the 24-hour, 50-minute rhythm of the tides. You are probably most alert first thing in the morning and find your brain skills bottoming out by nightfall.
- You can go longer without food than you can without sleep. Deprived of sleep it would only be a matter of days before you started to get headaches, dizziness, sickness, confusion and other problems. Death would soon follow.
- When you were a baby, you needed 20 hours of sleep in a 24-hour cycle; as an adult you will need 7 to 8. Different creatures need different amounts of sleep. The koala sleeps 22 hours a day; bats and sloths, 20; opossums, 19; armadillos, 17; hamsters, 15; chimpanzees, 14; cats, 12; pigs, 8; cows, 4; donkeys and horses, 3; giraffes, 2.
- You don't stay still when you are sleeping. If you did, you would squish the nerves, blood vessels and other body parts you are sleeping on. You change your position an average of 32 times per night.